WHICH
NEW ZEALAND
BIRD?

A Simple Step-by-Step Guide to the Identification of
New Zealand's Native & Introduced Birds

Andrew Crowe
Illustrated by Dave Gunson

PENGUIN

Introduction

Which birds are covered?
Although more than 320 species of bird have been seen in New Zealand, many of these were birds blown here during a storm. Some have only ever been seen here once. Over 100 are similar looking ocean birds and more than thirty are rare visiting waders. For simplicity, this book covers only those 96 birds the beginner is likely to see – birds likely to be spotted in the wild or those in special wildlife sanctuaries.

Māori & birds
When native birds were plentiful, most kinds were hunted by Māori for food. Bird feathers were used for decorating cloaks, canoes and food containers, as headbands or simply worn in the hair or made into earrings. Some cloaks were made from the bird skins themselves. Feathers were also worn like a moustache, inserted sideways through a hole made in that part of the nose which separates the nostrils. Feathers made useful paint brushes too. Black-backed gulls were used for pest control in kūmara gardens, while other birds brought warning of coming storms, signalled the arrival of the seasons, or were used in rituals, particularly in love charms and the blessing of children. Two native birds (kākā and tūī) even provided Māori with caged pets which they taught to speak. Birds formed a large part of Māori lore and culture, with over 760 specific names being given to them (see page 94), many of these subsequently entering into English, eg kiwi, tūī, kākā, kea, pūkeko, weka.

Perhaps the most intriguing part birds played in New Zealand history is the fact that the regular migratory flights of the long-tailed cuckoo are credited with leading to the original Polynesian discovery of New Zealand.

Birds special to New Zealand
Since people arrived in New Zealand, at least forty native birds have become extinct, yet this country remains remarkable for its huge number of unique birds. Indeed, 60 per cent of our native land and fresh water birds, and 30 per cent of the seabirds are found nowhere else.

Native or introduced?
In this book, each bird is given a clear, colour-coded label to show whether it is:

Native
& found only in New Zealand
Endemic: a bird which *breeds only in New Zealand*.

Native
Native: a bird which has *found its own way to New Zealand* without human help and now breeds here in the wild.

Introduced
Introduced: a bird which was *brought here by people* and now breeds here in the wild.

Regular Visitor
Migrant: a bird which breeds overseas, but *visits New Zealand* every year to feed during our summer.

What the little numbers mean
Each bird is labelled (next to the map) to show how common it is:

| Very common (100) | Common (40) | Quite common (15) | Not common (8) | Rare (1) | Sanctuary bird (0) |

The numbers show how likely you are to see the bird in the wild. '100' is as easy to find as a blackbird. '0' means it is so rare you will only see it in a bird sanctuary.

These numbers* should help the beginner to see why, for example, a yellow bird is far more likely to be a yellowhammer (70) than a yellowhead (1). Or a hawk-like bird is more likely to be an Australasian harrier (75) than a New Zealand falcon (6).

---

* The numbers are calculated from a national survey by over 800 ornithologists 1969-1979. These numbers do not represent the population sizes of these birds; they simply indicate how many times a particular bird was reported during the period of the survey.

How to identify a bird using this book

STEP ONE: WHERE DID YOU SEE IT?

The birds are found in six main habitats, listed below. Turn straight to the appropriate section and check the picture key(s) at the beginning of that section.

Go to Page

Forest Birds
Birds found in mature forest – native or exotic. (For scrub, go to page 35.) **4**

Sanctuary Birds
Birds seen only on sanctuary islands or at special wildlife centres **22**

Mountain Birds
Birds found in the mountains – above the tree line **26**

Countryside & Garden Birds
Birds found in towns, parks, gardens, orchards, farmland, scrub or on roadsides **30**

Freshwater Birds
Birds found on lakes, swamps or rivers **50**

Seashore Birds
Birds found on beaches, rocky shores or estuaries **67**

STEP TWO: HOW BIG WAS IT?

Birds are arranged in each section by weight, from the smallest to the largest. The weight and length of each bird is given (from the tip of its bill to the tip of its tail). Where male and female birds are different sizes, the male size is given first:

2200/2800g	40cm

STEP THREE: CHECK THE IDENTIFICATION TIPS

The most useful identification tips are listed. Identification tips in italics draw attention to the various forms of a species and show how to distinguish the bird in question from a similar species.

STEP FOUR: TROUBLESHOOTING

If you are having any trouble with this approach, don't give up! Ask yourself:
(1) **Is the bird a striking colour?** If so, go to page 87.
(2) If not, **Does it have a very long bill, neck, legs or tail?** If so, go to page 87.
(3) If not, then go straight to **Birds by Size** on page 86 (listing all the birds in this book).
(4) If you are still puzzled, **A Simple Key to Bird Groups** is provided on page 88.
(5) On the other hand, if you cannot see the bird but can only hear its call, go to the beginning of the appropriate habitat section: **Birds often Found by their Call** (pages 5, 26, 31, 50, 67).

What the symbols mean

Shading shows where the bird is found within the main islands of New Zealand.

Binoculars are particularly useful with this habitat or bird.

A bird which is active at night.

Forest Birds

(Birds found in mature native forest & pine forest)

Most birds found in New Zealand forest are native, and most of these are not found in any other country (endemic). Yet, surprisingly, a few introduced birds are also common here, even a long way inside mature native forests. Since the beginner will not know which birds are native and which are introduced, both are shown together in the picture key on the following pages.

A walk into forest often takes you first through areas of **low scrub**, or regenerating forest. This land has usually been burnt in the past to clear it for farming. Here, introduced birds – especially finches – are more common. *For these scrubland birds, go to the farmland picture key on page 35.*

TIPS for Birdwatching in Forest

◆ Old-growth forests often support a better range of native birds, especially in areas where predators are being controlled. Recommended places for seeing forest birds are shown in green on the birdwatching hot spots map (page 92).

◆ Clearings or breaks in the forest are often easier places to spot birds.

◆ Check out the forest canopy from above, eg from a cliff, bridge or tower. You will often see different birds here – either birds which prefer to feed in the tree tops, or birds flying over the forest canopy – see pages 6 and 7.

◆ Listen for calls or movement and use binoculars for canopy birds. You will see more birds if you keep still and quiet for five minutes.

◆ Try birdwatching in forest at night (for kiwi or morepork). Take a good torch. So as not to frighten kiwi, cover the light with red cellophane.

◆ Mature, pruned, pine forest will often have a good range of native birds, so long as there is a good understorey of native shrubs.

KEY: Forest Birds often Found by their Call

Many birds have a range of songs including special calls for raising the alarm, for finding a mate or establishing territory. Only common forest songs or calls are listed.

Forest Songbirds (Continuous song or melody. Most native songbirds sing throughout the year)

	page	
Grey Warbler	8	An energetic, warbling trill (male)
Fantail	9	'Tweet-a-tweet-a-tweet-a-tweet' (& 'cheet, cheet, cheet')
Tomtit	9	Descending warble: 'sweedle-sweedle-sweedle-u-swee' (male)
Brown Creeper	10	High-pitched: 'roh-ree-roh-ree-ree' (not in the North Island) (male)
Silvereye	10	Quiet warble, trills and slurs (& '**z**irp')
Whitehead	11	High-pitched: 'swee-swee-swee-chir-chir' (North Island only) (male)
Shining Cuckoo	12	Tu**wee** tu**wee** tu**wee** tu**wee** tu**wee tiw**oo' (late spring & early summer)
Bellbird	13	'Plink, plonk, plock, plink, plonk ...' (no grunts, coughs or chortles)
NZ Robin	13	Loud descending warble: 't**wee**p-t**wee**p-t**wee**p-too-too-too' (& 'tok, tok, tok')
Tūī	15	Liquid bell notes with grunts, coughs & chortles (also mimics other birds)

Daytime Forest Shrieks & Screeches

	page	
Parakeet	14	Fast, high-pitched chattering cry: 'kita-kita-kita-kita'
Long-Tailed Cuckoo	16	A piercing screech: 'zzwhoo**eesh**t' (late spring & summer)
Falcon	17	Shrill scream: '**keek-keek-keek-keek-keek**'
Kākā	18	Screeching: '**kra, kra, ka**' (also liquid whistling song)

Other Simple Daytime Forest Calls (Not musical)

	page	
Rifleman	8	Simple, quiet, very high squeak: 'zit-zit-zit' (like twisting a cork in a bottle)
Fernbird	54	'**Utik utik utik**' (bird hidden in low scrub)
Kingfisher	55	Loud: '**weet-weet-weet-weet**'
Weka	20	'Coo**eet**-coo**eet**-coo**eet**-coo**eet**-coo**eet**' (mostly South Island)

Forest Night Calls (Note that possums also make grunts, screeches and hisses at night.)

	page	
Long-Tailed Cuckoo	16	A piercing screech: 'zzwhoo**eesh**t' (late spring & summer)
Morepork	16	'**More pork**' repeated (also '**krree**' & hooting calls)
Kākā	18	Screeching: '**kra, kra, ka**' (also liquid whistling song)
Weka	20	'Coo**eet**-coo**eet**-coo**eet**-coo**eet**-coo**eet**' (mostly South Island)
Kiwi (male)	21	A long series of shrill whistles: 'ki**weee**e, ki**weee**e ...'
Kiwi (female)	21	Series of harsh screeches: 'zk**u**wee, zk**u**wee ...'

KEY: FOREST BIRDS (For scrubland birds, go to page 35.)

The birds are placed in the picture according to where they are most likely to be *first* seen. Many are equally at home at several levels. **They are arranged in order of size, with the smallest bird in each group at the left.**

Flying over forest

Tūī	Falcon	Kākā	NZ Pigeon	Harrier
page 15	page 17	page 18	page 19	page 48

Usually only spotted high in the trees

(North Island only)   (spring & summer)   (South Island only)

Whitehead	Shining Cuckoo	Yellowhead	Bellbird	Parakeet	Kingfisher	Tūī	Rosella
page 11	page 12	page 12	page 13	page 14	page 55	page 15	page 44

Usually seen near head height

(South Island only)   (at night)

Rifleman	Grey Warbler	Fantail	Tomtit	Brown Creeper	Silvereye	Bellbird	Morepork
page 8	page 8	page 9	page 9	page 10	page 10	page 13	page 16

Seen on, or near, the ground

(mostly South Island) (at night)

Dunnock	Chaffinch	NZ Robin	Thrush	Blackbird	Weka	Kiwi
page 38	page 38	page 13	page 42	page 43	page 20	page 21

(spring & summer)   (North Island only)

Long-T Cuckoo
page 16

Kōkako
page 17

Kākā
page 18

NZ Pigeon
page 19

Rifleman / Tītīpounamu

Acanthisitta chloris [Acanthisittidae]

Native	
& found only in New Zealand	
Common in places (15)	
6/7g	8cm

♦ Call: high-pitched 'zit, zit, zit'
♦ Hops up tree trunks (*unlike warbler*)
♦ Flicks its wings

♦ Appears to have no tail (*unlike warbler – below*)

FEMALE

♦ Long thin bill curved slightly upward

MALE

The mouse-sized rifleman is New Zealand's smallest bird. It is not well known, for its usual home is old, high-altitude beech forest, where it is seen hopping in a spiral up the trunks of trees, picking off insects and spiders. The rifleman usually nests in holes in trees – the same mature trees which are often chosen during selective logging of native forests. Both European and Māori common names refer to the colouring of the male bird, for the uniforms of 19th century military riflemen were olive green, similar to the colour of pounamu (greenstone). The bird's call is no louder than the song of a cricket and often too high-pitched for older people to hear. But you can attract it by rubbing a piece of cork on a wet bottle. Good spots to find them include Pureora Forest, Pukeiti Rhododendron Reserve near New Plymouth, Lake Rotopounamu, the Waikareiti Track near Lake Waikaremoana, at Day's Bay in Wellington, in the Dunedin Reserves, at Arthur's Pass, and in the Eglinton Valley. Found only in New Zealand, with two similar subspecies, the South Island one being the more common. Can live to at least 6 years old.

Grey Warbler / Riroriro

Gerygone igata [Acanthizidae]

Native	
& found only in New Zealand	
Very common (75)	
6.5g	10cm

♦ Hovers. Never seems to sit still
♦ Heard more often than seen
♦ Male song: a long warbling trill

♦ Dark tail feathers with white tips (*unlike rifleman & silvereye*)

The restless grey warbler builds a remarkably neat, hanging pear-shaped nest with a roof and a small round opening on one side – a nest design which may help to protect these birds from rats. Even so, the warbler often manages to raise just one batch of chicks, for it is then that the **shining cuckoo** (page 12) arrives from the Solomon Islands to lay its own eggs in the warbler's nest.

At just a few days old, the faster-growing (but still naked) cuckoo chick tips out all the warbler eggs and chicks. In their place, the warbler parents raise a young cuckoo. The warbler sings all year, but mostly in spring and summer – providing a useful signal to early Māori to start preparing the ground for planting. It is not until this song is slowed down on tape, that its remarkable complexity can be appreciated by the human ear. Warblers are very common in forests, scrub and gardens, where they eat mostly insects and spiders. Can live to about 10 years old. Several similar warblers live in Australia but this one is found only in New Zealand. (The Chatham Islands have their own species.)

Fantail / Pīwakawaka

Rhipidura fuliginosa [Monarchidae]

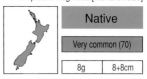

Native		
Very common (70)		
8g	8+8cm	

◆ Very long fanned tail (as long as body)

◆ Friendly. Flies like a butterfly
◆ Call: 'cheet, cheet'

One of New Zealand's best-known and most-loved birds, the fantail is common in forest, scrub and gardens – anywhere there are trees. It often enters houses in summer, looking for flies and enjoys bathing in the spray from a garden hose. It has been known to settle on people's shoulders, their head or even on an outstretched hand. Try attracting one by rubbing a piece of polystyrene or cork on a wet bottle. It is fun to watch its restless flight as it stops in mid-air, suddenly switching direction to snap up flying insects (including sandflies) with a click of its bill. These jerky movements led Māori to describe a restless person as being like a fantail. The fantail's neat, cup-shaped nest is often noticed as it is frequently built near head-height. Other subspecies of the same bird are found in Australia and on some western Pacific Islands. There are three similar subspecies in New Zealand, the South Island one sometimes completely black. The odd bird can likewise be completely white (albino), though this is rare. The oldest bird found in New Zealand was 3 years old, but in Australia they can live to 10 years.

Tomtit / Miromiro

Petroica macrocephala [Eopsaltriidae]

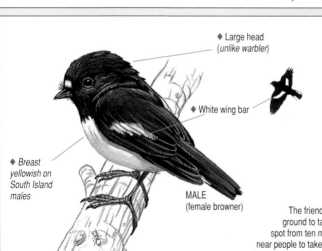

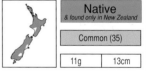

Native		
& found only in New Zealand		
Common (35)		
11g	13cm	

◆ Large head (*unlike warbler*)

◆ White wing bar

◆ Breast yellowish on South Island males

MALE (female browner)

◆ Friendly. Often flies to the ground
◆ Often clings to tree trunks, head down
◆ *Smaller than NZ robin (page 13)*
◆ Male sings a descending warble: 'sweedle-sweedle-sweedle-u-swee'

The friendly tomtit often flies from a low perch to the ground to take insects, spiders or worms, which it can spot from ten metres away. Tomtits will sometimes gather near people to take insect food which might be disturbed by a tramper's boot. They have even been known to sit on people's shoulders, as if to whisper a message. To Māori it was indeed a love messenger and its song signalled the changing seasons. It can be attracted by squeaking a piece of cork or polystyrene over wet glass and is most common in mature native beech forest, along the western side of the South Island. Other easy places to find them include Opepe Historic Reserve (near Taupo), Kapiti Island, Arthur's Pass, Eglinton Valley and Stewart Island. Also called pied tit (North Island) or (in the South Island) ngiru-ngiru or yellow-breasted tit. Tomtits are thought to be able to live 10 years. Found only in New Zealand, with five similar subspecies. The Chatham Island one helped save the **black robin** from extinction by incubating any spare eggs given to it by conservation workers.

Brown Creeper / Pīpipi

Mohoua novaeseelandiae [Pachycephalidae]

Native	
& found only in New Zealand	
Common in places (10)	
13/11g	13cm

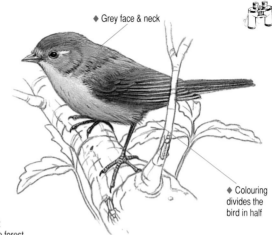

♦ Grey face & neck

♦ Colouring divides the bird in half

- ♦ **Not in the North Island**
- ♦ Often spotted near head height
- ♦ Flocks feed noisily, high in the trees
- ♦ Male song high-pitched, canary-like: 'roh-ree-roh-ree-ree'

Found only in the South Island and Stewart Island, mostly in native forest and in pine forest, but sometimes in scrub too. Its common name refers to the way the bird moves over tree trunks looking for insects. Like the related whitehead and yellowhead, it often forms small, noisy, fast-moving flocks high in the forest canopy, where it feeds on insects. The brown creeper can be hard to see without binoculars but can sometimes be attracted by squeaking a piece of polystyrene or cork on a wet bottle. Only the female incubates the eggs. In November or December, the **long-tailed cuckoo** (page 16) will often lay its egg in the nest too. The brown creeper is left to raise the cuckoo's young. The strange chick soon dwarfs its foster parent, eventually reaching ten times its weight! Good places to find brown creepers include forest patches on Bank's Peninsula, around Dunedin, along the West Coast, Arthur's Pass, Lake Gunn in the Eglinton Valley, and Stewart Island.

Silvereye / Tauhou

Zosterops lateralis [Zosteropidae]

Native
Very common (70)

13g	12cm

♦ Bright olive green above

♦ White eye-ring

- ♦ Forms noisy flocks in winter
- ♦ Quiet song

Most New Zealanders know this bird as the white-eye or waxeye, from its distinctive white eye-ring. Māori named it 'tauhou', meaning 'stranger', for the silvereye appears to have arrived here from Australia as recently as 1832. (It is found also in the south-western Pacific.) Its arrival is believed to have had a big impact on the availability of foods for other native forest birds, particularly tūī and bellbird, yet the silvereye has become an important flower pollinator and carrier of small forest seeds. Like the tūī, it has a brush-like tongue for taking nectar. The birds eat woolly aphids too (which used to be a problem on apple trees) so they were also known as blightbirds. By whatever name, it is a familiar bird anywhere where there are trees – in gardens, orchards, scrub and forest. The silvereye builds a neat, cup-shaped nest which it hangs like a hammock between twigs or leaves. Over a 14-hour day, parents may feed their young over 250 times. Besides nectar and insects, they also eat spiders and fruit. In winter, they are easily attracted to gardens with a piece of apple or a tin of cooking fat on a bird table. They also like bird baths. To fruit-growers, they can be both helpful and a nuisance, depending on whether they are feeding on insect pests or pecking at their fruit. A small flock of silvereyes was recently spotted from a ship 600 km east of New Zealand – destination unknown. Can live to over 11 years old.

Whitehead / Pōpokotea

Mohoua albicilla [Pachycephalidae]

Native
& found only in New Zealand
Not common (6)

18/14g	15cm

◆ **In North Island forest only**
◆ Flocks feed noisily, high in the trees
◆ Very fast-moving
◆ Canary-like song: 'swee-swee-swee-chir-chir' (male)

◆ White head & belly
(more obvious on males)

The whitehead is found only in the North Island – in both native forest and mature pine forest. It is not common and is hard to see without binoculars, for the whitehead spends most of its time in the very tops of the trees, eating insects and spiders (and some berries). Its cup-shaped nest is usually built in the tree-tops too. In summer, autumn and winter, whiteheads fly in noisy, fast-moving flocks of up to thirty birds. To Māori, these flocks were a warning that ghosts (kehua) were about. In November and December, the **long-tailed cuckoo** (page 16) often lays its egg in the whitehead's nest, leaving the whitehead to raise a chick which will eventually grow to seven times the weight of its foster parent! Good spots to find whitehead include Tiritiri Matangi Island, the 'Forest Tower' at Pureora Forest, the pine forests of central North Island (eg Atiamuri), Opepe Historic Reserve (near Taupo), Lake Rotopounamu, Kapiti Island and Karori Wildlife Sanctuary. The birds can be attracted by squeaking a piece of polystyrene or cork on a wet bottle. It is closely related to the yellowhead and brown creeper. Can live to over 8 years old. (The Māori name is sometimes misspelled 'pōpokatea'.)

Chaffinch / Pahirini

(Very common on the forest floor)
Go to page 38

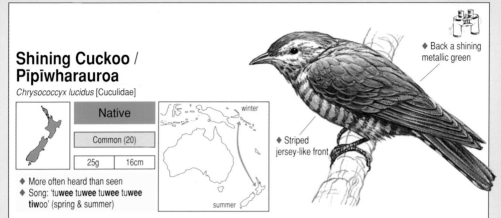

Shining Cuckoo / Pīpīwharauroa

Chrysococcyx lucidus [Cuculidae]

Native
Common (20)

25g	16cm

- Back a shining metallic green
- Striped jersey-like front

◆ More often heard than seen
◆ Song: 'tu**wee** tu**wee** tu**wee** tu**wee** ti**w**oo' (spring & summer)

(map: winter / summer)

The shining cuckoo is an extraordinary traveller, spending winter in Papua New Guinea, Indonesia and the Solomon Islands. In spring, it heads south over vast stretches of ocean to breed, arriving back in New Zealand in late September and early October. It begins laying its green eggs in November – but not in nests of its own. In just ten seconds it pops its egg into the nest of a grey warbler, replacing one of the warbler's own eggs. When still just a few days old, the cuckoo chick – still naked and blind – uses a hollow in its back to tip out the rest of the warbler's eggs or chicks from the nest. At the end of summer, the shining cuckoo flies north on a 3,500 km-journey, which the young manage to navigate without any help for they have apparently never even met their parents. On returning to New Zealand, they often come back to the same spot where they were born. Here, the cuckoo lives in forest, scrub and gardens, yet is rarely seen, for its green colouring is good camouflage. It is easiest to spot in farm willow trees or gum trees, or when one stuns itself by flying into a window. It feeds on insects, particularly kōwhai moth and 'woolly bear' caterpillars. Some Māori explained its sudden appearance with the belief that the bird's parents were really tree lizards, while others knew it arrived from the warmer north. Each year, its arrival signalled the fourth month of their calendar, the time to begin spring planting. Māori valued its feathers highly and would present boxes of them as gifts. The shining cuckoo is found also in Australia, Vanuatu and New Caledonia.

Yellowhead / Mohua

Mohoua ochrocephala [Pachycephalidae]

Native
& found only in New Zealand

Rare (1)

30/25g	15cm

◆ **In South Island forest only**
◆ Flocks feed noisily high in the trees (except in spring & early summer)
◆ Canary-like song, with buzzes (male)

◆ Bright yellow head & belly

This rare and attractive bird is found only in the South Island, in mature native forest, especially beech. Unlike the common yellowhammer (page 39), it is never found in open country. A good place to see them is in the roadside forests of the Eglinton Valley, Lake Gunn Track and at Haast Pass. On the eastern side, they can be seen on the Catlins River Walk. From mid-summer to the end of winter, they gather into flocks of up to 25 birds roaming the tree tops, often along with other species of forest birds. They can be very hard to see without binoculars, but can be attracted by squeaking a piece of polystyrene on a glass bottle. The yellowhead nests in holes in old trees, so will benefit from an end to selective logging. It feeds on insects and spiders, often using its tail feathers as a support when feeding on the trunk of a tree. This is why its tail feathers often look worn and untidy. The long-tailed cuckoo (page 16) sometimes lays its egg in a yellowhead nest. Also known as bush canary. Can live to at least 12 years old. An illustration of it appears on the NZ $100 note.

◆ Long tail, slightly forked

◆ Olive green bird *(female has a duller colour & a white stripe below the eye)*

◆ Curved bill

Bellbird / Korimako

Anthornis melanura [Meliphagidae]

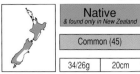

Native
& found only in New Zealand

Common (45)

34/26g	20cm

◆ Song: bell-like (with no grunts, coughs or chortles)
◆ Fast, noisy, whirring flight
◆ Rare in Waikato & Northland

'Like the bellbird's song at dawn' is a traditional Māori way to describe a particularly good speaker or singer. At dawn and dusk, the eloquent song of korimako can sound like ringing bells or like flutes playing. Unlike European songbirds, both the male and female birds sing – and throughout the year. When hunting them, Māori used a 'call-leaf' to attract the bird, placing a flat or doubled leaf between their lips and sucking air to make a chirping sound. The same can be done with a piece of polystyrene rubbed on wet glass. Found mostly in forest, but sometimes in scrub and gardens, especially in the South Island. The bellbird was given legal protection in 1896, at a time when the bird seemed to be dying out – probably because of rats. It has since recovered and, yet, it is still rare in the Waikato or north of Auckland, except in winter when the odd male flies over from one of the off-shore islands. Like the tūī, it is an important pollinator of native forest flowers and carrier of small seeds, often behaving like an acrobat while it feeds on nectar, honeydew, insects and fruit. Both birds belong to the same family as the honeyeaters of Australia, all of which have a brush-like tongue which is useful when drinking nectar. Can live to over 8 years old. Four subspecies in New Zealand.

◆ Large head

◆ *South Island males have a cream chest*

◆ Very long thin legs, standing very upright *(unlike tomtit – page 9)*

NZ Robin / Toutouwai

Petroica australis [Eopsaltriidae]

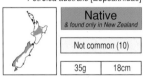

Native
& found only in New Zealand

Not common (10)

35g	18cm

◆ Friendly & curious
◆ Hops about on the ground
◆ Call: a soft 'tok, tok, tok'
◆ Male song: 'tw**ee**p-tw**ee**p-tw**ee**p-too-too-too'

The friendly long-legged robin usually perches on a low branch or tree trunk, flying to the forest floor to catch insects and worms. Try attracting it by scraping back some leaf litter with your foot to help it find insects and worms. Take a few steps back and wait. They have even been known to land on people's heads or boots or to feed from their hands. It sometimes hops on the forest floor, trembling one leg to bring insects to the surface or picks up millipedes to brush on its feathers as an insecticide. The New Zealand robin is found among old trees in both native and pine forests. Good spots to see them include Tiritiri Matangi Island, forests around the Rotorua Lakes and Taupo, Kapiti Island, Karori Wildlife Sanctuary, Arthur's Pass and in the Eglinton Valley. Also known to Māori as 'pītoitoi' after the bird's song, described as 'pi-toi-toi-toi!' Early settlers gave it the European name after the similar-looking (but unrelated) European robin red-breast. Although similar 'robins' are found in Australia, this one is found only in New Zealand, with three similar subspecies, one for each of the main islands. The New Zealand robin can live to over 16 years old. The famous **black robin**, rescued from the brink of extinction in the 1980s, is found only on the Chatham Islands. It looks similar, but is a different species.

For easy comparison, the colour art on these two pages is all to the same scale: HALF LIFE-SIZE

Yellow-Crowned Parakeet / Kākāriki

Cyanoramphus auriceps [Psittacidae]

Native
& found only in New Zealand

Not common (6)

50/40g	25/23cm

- ◆ *Half the weight of a rosella (page 44)*
- ◆ In the tree tops of mature forest
- ◆ High-pitched cry: 'kita-kita-kita-kita'

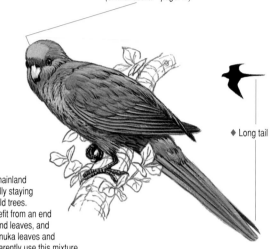

◆ Yellow crown with red band
(unlike rosella – page 44)

◆ Long tail

Native parakeets are so rarely seen nowadays that it is hard to picture the tens of thousands of birds which would arrive like 'an army of locusts' in farmland as the settlers' corn ripened. Today, mainland birds are found only in mature native forest, usually staying high up in the trees, where they nest in holes in old trees. Hence, these are among the birds which will benefit from an end to selective logging. They eat fruit, seeds, buds and leaves, and can sometimes be seen chewing kānuka and mānuka leaves and branches to spread over their feathers. They apparently use this mixture to control lice in their feathers, as the *leptospermone* these leaves contain is a known insecticide. Yellow-crowned parakeets are most common in South Island beech forests. In the North Island, they follow flocks of whitehead; in the South Island, they are often seen with yellowhead. Good spots to see them include the forest tower at Pureora Forest, the Eglinton Valley and nearby Rees, Dart and Routeburn Tracks and on Stewart Island. Māori hunted the birds for food and for their vivid green feathers which decorated many flax cloaks, sometimes keeping live birds as decoys, tying them first through the beak with a cord. The Māori name 'kākāriki' means 'small parrot' but is also the word for the colour green. In Māori lore, the bird was still more colourful before kākā stole most of its red feathers for the underneath of its own wings. Early settlers frequently kept them as talking pets. An orange-fronted form is sometimes seen in North Canterbury and a similar subspecies is found on the Chatham Islands. The slightly larger **red-crowned parakeet** (*C. novaezelandiae*) is rare on the main islands but can be seen on Tiritiri Matangi, Kapiti and Stewart Islands. (See also page 22.)

Kingfisher / Kōtare

(Often heard in the tree tops but hard to see here.)
Go to page 55

Blackbird / Manu Pango
(Very common on the forest floor)
Go to page 43

Tūī
Prosthemadera novaeseelandiae
[Meliphagidae]

Native	
& found only in New Zealand	
Common (40)	
120/90g	30cm

♦ Song: loud & very varied, including grunts, coughs & gurgles
♦ Fast, noisy flier, with whirring wingbeats, often gliding or diving with closed wings

♦ White wing bars seen in flight

♦ Pair of white throat tufts on adult bird *(unlike blackbird – above)*

These remarkable songsters were kept by Māori in cages made with mānuka twigs or with supplejack vines and flax leaves and trained to memorise and repeat elaborate Māori welcome speeches of up to seventy words or more. The bristles of the bird's brush-like tongue would even be trimmed, as this apparently helped the bird speak more clearly. But the natural voice of the tūī is unforgettable too: a very varied, liquid song with grunts, coughs and chortles, including some notes, at about 21 kilohertz, that are too high for the human ear. It is said to be able to imitate the call of every bird in the forest, as well as turkeys, geese, crowing roosters, cats, barking dogs, the cough of an old man, or a child's laughter – even the 'beep-beep' of a modern car alarm. It is the first bird to sing in the morning and last to finish at night. On bright, moonlit nights, it sometimes just keeps going. Both male and female birds sing. Although the tūī is often heard in native forest, it is usually easier to see in gardens with flowering trees or flax. It takes nectar from kōwhai, flax and rātā flowers, but also eats fruit and insects. It is attracted to gardens by flowering gums or sugar water put out for them, often noisily chasing other birds away. Māori attracted tūī with chirping sounds made by sucking breath over a folded leaf such as tūrutu (blueberry) or patē (seven finger), hunting the birds for food and for its feathers which were used to decorate woven flax cloaks, caps and food containers. Early bushmen ate them too, sometimes using both the tūī and kererū to stuff pigs. Hundreds of skins were also exported to London to decorate ladies' hats. Since 1873, it has been a protected bird. The tūī is an important pollinator of native forest flowers and carrier of small seeds. Its noisy flight is due to a notch in one of its outer wing feathers, making that feather flutter. Can live to over 12 years old. The Chatham Islands have their own subspecies.

Long-Tailed Cuckoo / Koekoeā
Eudynamys taitensis [Cuculidae]

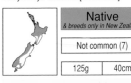

Native	
& breeds only in New Zealand	

Not common (7)	
125g	40cm

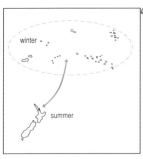

winter

summer

◆ Makes a piercing screech late spring & summer: 'zzwhoo**eesht**' (even at night)
◆ Seen in tree tops in the same forests as whitehead, brown creeper & yellowhead

◆ Very long tail *(far longer than on NZ falcon – opposite)*

◆ Pale bars & spots

The migrations of this bird are believed to have helped Māori discover New Zealand; indeed, there are even tales of this cuckoo being used to carry knotted cords for long-distance communication. The long-tailed cuckoo is found in tall forest, near the tops of the trees. It never builds a nest but lays its eggs instead in the nests of whitehead, brown creeper or yellowhead. It breeds only in New Zealand, but spends winter in the tropical Pacific, mostly east of Fiji, arriving back here (at the same spot!) in early October. Most birds will have left New Zealand again on their long journey north by early March. Each year, the birds travel about 3,500 km each way at speeds of up to 80 km/hr on a vast ocean journey which the young manage to navigate without any help, for they have apparently never even met their parents. Those flying to Palau Island (Belau), off the coast of the Philippines, will travel over 6,000 km. The long-tailed cuckoo eats insects, lizards, small birds and other birds' eggs. Māori caught them for their long tail feathers and speckled brown breast feathers, which were used in making cloaks or caps. Good spots to find the birds include forested stretches of the Wanganui River, tall forests in central North Island and Westland, Kapiti Island, Eglinton Valley and Stewart Island. A similar bird (the koel) is found in Australia.

Morepork / Ruru
Ninox novaeseelandiae [Strigidae]

Native	

Quite common (15)	
175g	29cm

◆ Large, staring eyes

◆ Heard at night; seldom seen (except when hunting near lights)
◆ Call: '**more pork**', a screeching '**krree**' or hooting calls

Although New Zealand's only native owl is fairly common in forest, scrub and gardens, it is not often seen as it sleeps during the day on a well-hidden branch, in a hole – or fork – of a tree. At late dusk, its silhouette can sometimes be seen around outdoor lights, even in large cities like Auckland, where it silently swoops for large moths and flying beetles. It also hunts small birds, mice, rats and lizards. Its remarkably silent flight is due to soft feathers along the edges of its wings. For night-time hunting, it has very large eyes at the front of its head and can turn its neck 270°. It has exceptional hearing too, due partly to the disks around its eyes which channel sound to its large ears. Moreporks were destroyed by early settlers who saw these birds attacking their newly-introduced chaffinches and skylarks – overlooking the fact that the owl also helped to control rats, mice and insect pests. The morepork has a wide range of calls, some of which were taken by Māori as signs of bad luck – a belief about owls common throughout much of the world. Just as Europeans called it 'morepork' in imitation of its call, Māori named it 'ruru' or 'koukou'. A similar subspecies found on Norfolk Island was saved from extinction in 1987 when two New Zealand moreporks were taken there to mate with the last female. The southern boobook of Australia looks very similar but is now thought to be a different species. New Zealand's much larger native **laughing owl (whekau)** became extinct about 1914.

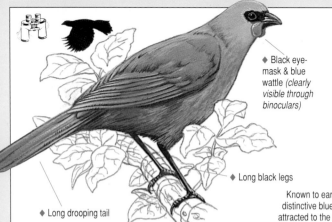

Kōkako

Callaeas cinerea [Callaeidae]

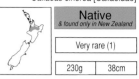

◆ Black eye-
mask & blue
wattle *(clearly
visible through
binoculars)*

Native	
& found only in New Zealand	
Very rare (1)	
230g	38cm

◆ **Not in South Island or Stewart Island**
◆ Heard mostly at dawn (rarely seen)
◆ Song: loud, sad organ-like notes
◆ Runs or leaps about in the tree tops
◆ *Twice the weight of a tūī (page 15)*

◆ Long black legs

◆ Long drooping tail

Known to early settlers as the blue-wattled crow, after the distinctive blue bags on its cheeks. The birds are strangely attracted to the sky blue forest mushroom (*Entoloma*) which shares the same colour and is known to Māori as werewere kōkako, or kōkako wattles. The kōkako is now so rare in the wild, that you are unlikely to come across it by chance. It lives in tall native forest, often staying high up in the trees, where it eats berries, leaves, fern fronds, flowers, buds and insects. Here, it balances on one leg like a parrot, eating food held by the other foot. It has become so rare partly because so much of its native lowland forest home has been destroyed for timber and farming. Video cameras have shown that the birds are often attacked on their nests by rats, possums and stoats. Although it has very small wings and rarely flies far, it will glide or use its very long legs to leap between branches or run like a squirrel. Its best chance for survival these days is on off-shore islands and 'mainland islands', where rats, possums and stoats are excluded or heavily controlled. The kōkako is thought to be able to live to over 20 years old. It was given legal protection in 1896. A good place to see them in the wild is Tiritiri Matangi Island, near Auckland. Its Māori name is an imitation of its call: 'ko-ka-ko-o-o-o'. Its song can be heard up to a kilometre away – a haunting sound not to be forgotten. Like the saddleback and extinct **huia**, the kōkako belongs to the wattlebird family. The orange-wattled South Island subspecies is now thought to be extinct, although some people continue to search for them just in case...

◆ Pointed wings
(unlike harrier)

HARRIER

FALCON

NZ Falcon / Kārearea

Falco novaeseelandiae [Falconidae]

Native	
& found only in New Zealand	
Not common (6)	
300/500g	43/47cm

◆ Tail shorter
than long-
tailed cuckoo
(opposite)

◆ Dark 'drooping
moustache'

◆ *Half the size of a harrier (page 48)*
◆ Swoops from perch. Seldom hovers
◆ Flies like a pigeon with fast wingbeats
◆ Shrill scream: **'keek-keek-keek-keek'**

Found mainly in forest and tussockland, but also in rough, high country farmland on the eastern side of the South Island. It is often confused with the harrier (page 48), but the harrier is twice the size of the falcon. The falcon is a formidable meat-eater with a hooked bill, powerful feet and strongly curved claws to grab its prey: large insects, birds, lizards, young rabbits and hares. Since the extinction of the giant **New Zealand eagle** (some 500 years ago) the falcon is by far the most aggressive bird of the forest, attacking and killing birds as large as the New Zealand pigeon, tūī, magpie, gull and even heron. It will even attack harrier in flight, turning on its back to strike its prey from underneath with its claws. Because of its taste for farm and game birds, it was shot by early settlers. In an attacking dive, it can reach speeds of up to 180 km/hr and attacks with its claws, not its bill, killing larger animals with a bite in the back of the neck. To help break up the food in its stomach, it swallows smooth pea-sized stones. Falcons nest on cliff ledges and among perching lilies, high in the forks of trees. Hence, it is another bird which will benefit from an end to selective logging. When nesting, they will sometimes defend their territory by making dive attacks on people. Trained falcons bred in captivity (under permit) have been used to scare away nuisance birds at airports. There are three forms of the species: the bush falcon, eastern falcon and southern falcon. Also known as sparrow hawk.

For easy comparison, the colour art on these two pages is all to the same scale: QUARTER LIFE-SIZE   **17**

♦ Large head & large bill

♦ Red underwings

Kākā
Nestor meridionalis [Psittacidae]

Native
& found only in New Zealand
Not common (9)
525/475g	45cm

♦ Noisy call: '**kra, kra, ka**' (day or
  night) & liquid whistling song
♦ Listen for falling bark & broken sticks
♦ Often seen flying over forest
♦ *Flight quieter & slower than a NZ pigeon – opposite*

This large parrot is usually seen in mature native forest, most commonly along the West Coast of the South Island, although the odd bird does find its way to such unlikely places as central Auckland. Easy places to see them include from the forest tower at Pureora Forest, Kapiti Island, Karori Wildlife Sanctuary, the Eglinton Valley and Stewart Island. They behave like monkeys, using their bills or feet to climb or swing through the branches. Kākā feed day and night, using their hooked bill to tear off loose bark and rotten wood to get at grubs. They like these so much that the birds can spend up to two hours digging to reach just one grub. A brush-like tongue helps them sip honeydew and nectar, but they also eat fruit, shoots and leaves. Because the kākā nests in old hollow trees, it is one of the birds to benefit from an end to selective logging which has damaged much old-growth forest. Off-shore islands, predator-free 'mainland islands' and wasp-proof feeding stations help to ensure the bird's long-term survival. Apart from being an important food of early Māori, its bright red underwing feathers were popular for decorating woven flax cloaks and caps. These kākā feather cloaks would be worn by the chiefs only, as more than 400 kākā could be killed to make just one cloak. European settlers used kākā feathers too, to stuff soft pillows, and hunted the birds for food, calling them by scratching a file over the edge of an old-style tin matchbox or tin can. Kākā were also kept as pets by Māori, tied with a piece of cord by one leg to a stick and taught to speak. Kākā were, however, never as fluent in Māori as tūī (page 15), for the tūī has a more complex 'voice box'. Such tame captive birds were also used as decoys when hunting. The common Māori name comes from the sound of the bird's call, but many other names were used, some referring to strangely-coloured birds, which can be creamy-white, canary yellow, red or brown. There are two subspecies, one in the South Island, one in the North. Some kākā live to over 20 years old.

◆ White 'singlet' or 'apron'

NZ Pigeon / Kererū
Hemiphaga novaeseelandiae [Columbidae]

| **Native** |
| *& found only in New Zealand* |

| Common (30) |

| 650g | 51cm |

◆ Heavy flight with slow, whooshing wingbeats, crashing clumsily through the branches
◆ Often seen flying over forest
◆ Makes stall dives in spring

Although not as spectacularly colourful as some of its Australian cousins, the kererū is still one of the world's most beautiful pigeons. It lives mostly in native forest, but in winter will sometimes fly up to 25 km to gardens to feed, not just on the fruits, flowers and leaves of native trees, but also on tree lucerne, broom, willow, poplar, guava, plum and privet. With the help of tiny radio transmitters attached to the birds, we now know that they eat the fruits of at least 70 species of plants, some birds covering a feeding range of up to 25 square kilometres. Kererū can swallow whole seeds the size of a twenty cent coin, so is the only bird which can spread the large seeds of trees like miro, matai, tawa, taraire, pūriri and karaka. So these trees all depend on the kererū for their survival. But bird numbers are dropping, partly due to illegal hunting, partly because of competition for food from rats and possums, and partly because the birds care for just one egg at a time, and this egg or chick is often eaten by rats, cats, possums or stoats. In spring and summer, adult birds can be seen flying steeply up into the sky until they run out of speed and then diving with stiffly held wings. These birds are showing off to each other to find a mate or telling one another that this is their territory. Both parents feed the young chick with a special 'pigeon milk' from inside their throats. To Māori, the bird's white breast represents the 'apron' of Taranga (Maui's mother). These white breast feathers and the olive green neck feathers were used for decorating cloaks, the colours being arranged in contrasting patterns. The body feathers were used for making cloaks and the tail feathers for decorating gourd bowls containing the cooked birds. Support for the pigeon's legal protection (since 1921) has not been wholehearted because of the place the bird holds within Māori tradition. But today, illegal hunting has become a serious threat to the bird's survival, particularly in Northland, where they are shot even during the breeding season. A breakdown of traditional values and a disrespect for rāhui (conservation measures) has led many to see the bird simply as free food to be shot with modern firearms, without any regard for the future. Given the chance, they may live to 10 years old or more, but these days such old birds are rare. One of its Māori names (kūkū) describes the bird's soft cry: 'ku-ku'. Other names include kūkupa (Northland and Stewart Island), parea (Chatham Islands) and wood pigeon. The Chatham Islands pigeon (parea) is a larger subspecies.

♦ Short bill *(unlike kiwi)*

♦ Very sturdy legs & feet

Weka
Gallirallus australis [Rallidae]

Native
& found only in New Zealand

Common in places (5)

1000/700g	53cm

♦ **Rare in the North Island**
♦ Cannot fly
♦ Runs fast with neck outstretched, or strides along with tail flicking
♦ Call: a series of rising 'coo**eet**s' (day or night)

The comical weka is a fast runner but, although it does have wings, it cannot fly. It lives mostly in forest and scrub, where it nests on the ground in a short burrow, in hollow logs or hidden under plants. The weka is so curious that it often walks long distances to visit picnic sites, bush camps and huts where it will steal just about anything – from watches to teaspoons (but also food). It flicks the leaf litter aside with its bill, not with its feet, eating a huge range of foods including eggs, rats, small birds, lizards, worms, snails, insects, seeds and fruit. For this reason, it often needs to be kept away from other endangered native wildlife. Like the city pigeon, it has a well-developed homing ability. In one experiment, a weka walked more than 300 km home; another swam 3 km in difficult seas. Weka were hunted by Māori and early Pākehā alike for food and oil, and South Island Māori used the skins to make capes and plucked its feathers to decorate flax cloaks. Māori called the birds by sucking air over a flax leaf or by using a young weka as a lure, and also hunted them with dogs. These days, the birds are eaten by cats, dogs and ferrets and continue to disappear from many areas, so volunteers are helping the birds by setting up captive breeding programmes. People setting possum bait stations can avoid accidental poisoning of such ground birds by placing the bait stations with the opening 70 cm above the ground (out of reach of both kiwi and weka). Given the chance, weka can live for over 15 years. The weka is believed to have originally flown to New Zealand as a wetland bird (similar to the banded rail), slowly evolving into a heavy forest bird with no need to fly. Up until a few hundred years ago, it would – along with the kiwi – have shared the forest floor with several similar flightless birds and several species of **moa**. Previously known as the woodhen, it belongs to the rail family and is hence related to the pūkeko and takahē. There are four subspecies in New Zealand. Easy places to see them include Kawau, Kapiti and Stewart Islands, Karori Wildlife Sanctuary and north-west South Island, where they can sometimes even be seen on the roadside. One little-known creature is totally dependant on the weka for its survival: the weka flea.

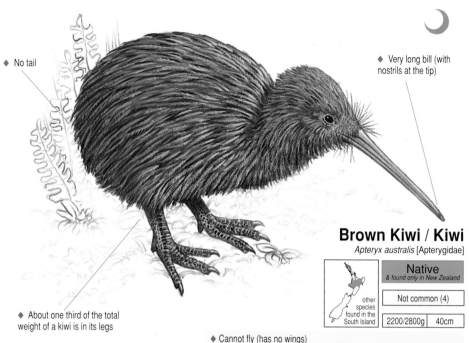

◆ No tail

◆ Very long bill (with nostrils at the tip)

Brown Kiwi / Kiwi
Apteryx australis [Apterygidae]

◆ About one third of the total weight of a kiwi is in its legs

Native
& found only in New Zealand

Not common (4)

2200/2800g	40cm

other species found in the South Island

◆ Cannot fly (has no wings)
◆ Active only at night *(except on Stewart Island)*
◆ Calls at night: 'ki**weee**' repeated 10-25 times, each call rising in pitch
◆ Snuffling sounds at night like a hedgehog

Few people have ever seen New Zealand's national emblem in the wild. Those who have, usually just get a glimpse of it by torchlight as its waddling backside shoots off into the undergrowth. Indeed, New Zealand's unique and most ancient bird lives more like a high-speed hedgehog than a bird, coming out from its burrow at night in forest, scrub and tussock. With nostrils at the tip of its bill, it is the only bird in the world known to be able to find food in the ground by smell. It eats mostly worms, but also insects (especially cicada nymphs) and fallen fruit. Yet kiwi have been seen eating the strangest things, like koura (freshwater crayfish) and frogs. Like a hedgehog, the kiwi makes snuffling sounds as it blows the soil out of its nostrils again. It is, as Māori say, 'te manu huna a Tane' (the hidden bird of Tane). Other signs of kiwi include large three-toed footprints and small holes in soft ground left by their probing bill. But it is the bird's loud night call which is most often noticed – about 40 minutes after sunset, when the bird comes out of its burrow. The male call sounds like the bird's Māori name: 'ki**weee**'. The bird's name comes from 'kivi', the Polynesian name for the bristle-thighed curlew, a shorebird with a similar call and a similarly long bill. The kiwi is a fast runner with large ears for good hearing. In spite of its small eyes, it has good night vision too (although it may be short-sighted). In its burrow, it lays either one or two large eggs and – in the North Island – it is the male which incubates them. For a bird of this weight, one would expect eggs the size of hen's eggs, but they are six times this size (see page 91). Kiwi were hunted by Māori not just for food but also for the long, hair-like feathers which were valued for covering woven flax cloaks and for decorating headbands. Europeans used their skins for making fashionable muffs and ate kiwi meat. The occasional bird can be part, or all, white (albino), which must be quite a nuisance for a bird which depends on camouflage for its survival. Since 1896, it has been a protected bird, but kiwi which have been accidentally killed are often donated to Māori for the continued traditional use of their feathers. They were hunted with dogs or called by making a hoarse whistle with one little finger in the mouth. Kiwi play an important rôle in spreading forest seeds, yet the population on the mainland is still dropping, largely due to dogs, stoats, ferrets, pigs, possums, possum traps and wild cats. People can help the birds by not letting their dogs roam in areas where kiwi still survive. In Northland, the birds are known to fall into cattle stops, get trapped and starve there. (A simple solution is to provide a ramp of road metal for them to climb out.) Remarkable research with radio transmitters in 1987, showed that one German shepherd dog killed 500 birds within a few months. Safe from such risks, they are thought to live to over 30 years old. Overall, the population has fallen from an estimated 12 million kiwi before humans arrived here to less than 70,000 now. They urgently need protected predator-free areas to survive. Even where they are heard in the wild, they are still hard to find, except perhaps at Aroha Island Ecological Reserve (Rangitane – page 92 & 93); also at Mason Bay on Stewart Island where tokoeka kiwi are often active during the day. By far the easiest place to see kiwi is in one of the special kiwi houses (see page 22) where artificial light at night has been used to reverse their day/night feeding cycle. There are at least four species, including **brown kiwi**, **tokoeka**, **great spotted kiwi** and **little spotted kiwi**. The brown kiwi is the most common of these. Kiwi are closely related to **moa**, ostrich and emu.

For easy comparison, the colour art on these two pages is to the same scale: QUARTER LIFE-SIZE

Sanctuary Birds

(Rare birds seen *only* in protected wildlife sanctuaries)

The four birds in this section are all special to New Zealand and are not found in any other country (endemic). They all now require protection within special wildlife sanctuaries to avoid extinction.

Such sanctuaries include off-shore islands such as Tiritiri Matangi, Little Barrier, Kapiti, Mana, Maud, Motuara and Codfish Islands, but also public wildlife display centres (see below).

Many of these centres are also good places to see kiwi, for, although kiwi (previous page) remain more common in the wild than any of the sanctuary birds in this section, it is still very hard to *actually find* wild kiwi. The same goes for **red-crowned parakeet** (mentioned on page 14) and **kōkako** (page 17).

Why are these sanctuary birds so rare? Partly because of the loss of their native forest habitat to logging and farming. But mainly because of pests brought to New Zealand by people. Mice, rats, wild cats, dogs, stoats, ferrets, weasels, hedgehogs, possums, deer and goats are all a threat to native birds as they either eat their eggs, chicks or the adult birds, or they compete for the same food.

WHERE to see New Zealand's Sanctuary Birds

There are no public displays of *kākāpō*. The easiest places to see the other sanctuary birds are listed below. (These places are shown on the birdwatching hot spots map on page 92.)

- Tiritiri Matangi Island *(stitchbird, saddleback & takahē)*.
- Mokoia Island in Lake Rotorua *(stitchbird & saddleback)*.
- Otorohanga Kiwi House *(saddleback)*.
- Mount Bruce Wildlife Centre *(stitchbird, saddleback & takahē)*.
- Kapiti Island *(stitchbird, saddleback & takahē)*.
- Karori Wildlife Sanctuary *(stitchbird, saddleback)*.
- Motuara Island *(saddleback)*.
- Te Anau Wildlife Centre *(takahē)*.
- Besides these centres and sanctuaries, there are kiwi houses in Kaitaia, Whangarei, Auckland, Rotorua, Waikanae, Wellington, Christchurch, Hokitika and Queenstown.

To see **black stilt**, visit the Black Stilt Aviary at Twizel. **Black robins** are found only in the Chatham Islands – on Mangere and Rangatira (South East) Islands.

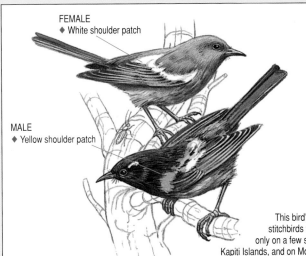

FEMALE
♦ White shoulder patch

MALE
♦ Yellow shoulder patch

Stitchbird / Hihi

Notiomystis cincta [Meliphagidae]

Native	
& found only in New Zealand	
Sanctuary bird (0)	
40/30g	18cm

♦ Larger than a sparrow
♦ Often seen in pairs
♦ Call: 'stit-stit-stit' or 'stitch'

This bird's name comes from its call. Until the early 1870s, stitchbirds were common in the North Island but now survive only on a few small islands, like Tiritiri Matangi, Little Barrier and Kapiti Islands, and on Mokoia Island in Lake Rotorua. Can now be seen at Karori Wildlife Sanctuary too, possibly now even in the Waitakere Ranges! The stitchbird eats nectar, fruit and some insects, often feeding near the ground. Flax flowers are a favourite. Like the bellbird and tūī, it is a 'honeyeater' with a brush-tipped tongue and, like those birds, it plays an important role in pollinating native forest flowers and carrying smaller seeds. Unlike most honeyeaters, though, it nests in holes in the trunks of trees. It is also the only bird in the world known to mate face to face. The female usually lays four white eggs which she incubates herself for about fifteen days, but when the time comes for feeding the chick, the male helps. Stitchbirds were hunted by Māori for food and for feathers for cloak-making, the bright yellow feathers of the male birds being especially popular. It was given legal protection in 1896. The stitchbird has never been found in the South Island. It can live for up to 7 years.

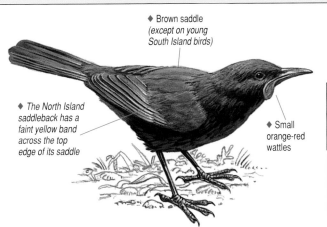

♦ Brown saddle
(except on young South Island birds)

♦ The North Island saddleback has a faint yellow band across the top edge of its saddle

♦ Small orange-red wattles

Saddleback / Tīeke

Philesturnus carunculatus [Callaeidae]

Native	
& found only in New Zealand	
Sanctuary bird (0)	
80/70g	25cm

♦ About the size of a blackbird
♦ Often seen on or near the ground
♦ Short flights; hops between branches or runs up branches
♦ Main call: a loud 'ke-eet, te-te-te-te'

There are two subspecies of saddleback, one found on offshore islands around the North Island, and a much rarer subspecies found on islands off the South Island. This South Island bird is one of the first birds in the world to be saved from extinction by people. In a daring move, braving rough seas, the few remaining birds were moved from rat-infested islands to rat-free off-shore islands by conservation workers in 1964. Today, saddlebacks can be most easily seen on Tiritiri Matangi and Little Barrier Islands, Mokoia Island in Lake Rotorua, on Kapiti and Motuara Islands and at the Karori Wildlife Sanctuary. It usually nests near the ground, often in holes in trees, where it lays two or three eggs. The saddleback eats insects and berries – often from the forest floor – using its strong, chisel-shaped bill to dig into rotting logs. It has a brush-tipped tongue too, which it uses for collecting nectar. The bird is named after the rusty brown 'saddle' on its back, a mark which, in Māori legend, was left by the scorching heat of Maui's hand. The saddleback was hunted for food, but given legal protection in 1896. It can live for over 17 years. Like the kōkako and extinct **huia**, it belongs to the wattlebird family – a family with no close relatives anywhere else in the world.

◆ Owl-like face

Kākāpō

Strigops habroptilus [Psittacidae]

Native
& found only in New Zealand

Sanctuary bird (0)

2500/2000g	63cm

- ◆ Male booms for hours at night
- ◆ Active mainly at night
- ◆ Cannot fly
- ◆ Sweet-smelling

Because of its strange diet and lifestyle, the kākāpō can be described as New Zealand's native equivalent of the rabbit. It is surely one of the world's rarest and strangest birds. Its Māori name ('night parrot') refers to the fact that the kākāpō hides among rotting logs during the day and comes out only at night. It is unusually heavy too – a record-breaker as the world's heaviest parrot. The male weighs up to 3.4 kg. Although a good runner and able to use its large wings to balance when climbing trees and vines, it cannot fly. With five ridges inside its upper bill to grind its food, it eats fruit, seeds, leaves, stems and roots. The way a kākāpō finds its mate is also very unusual. The males gather in groups on a hill-top, each bird sitting in a shallow pit in the ground, making very loud booming sounds throughout most of the night. These booms attract females from up to 7 km away; indeed its call is believed to carry further than that of any other bird in the world. The females visit the booming males only briefly and then go off on their own to nest on the ground (deep in a hollow log or tree stump), usually laying three smallish white eggs which they raise without any help from the males. The birds are thought to live for 30-50 years. Māori prized kākāpō feathers for making flax-and-feather cloaks, each of these cloaks requiring up to 11,000 feathers. The kākāpō was also one of the few birds skinned by Māori for making shoulder capes. These were described as sweet-smelling and remarkably warm. Indeed early European settlers valued these capes more than either mink or sable. Of course, such capes were usually moss green, but bright yellow kākāpō have also been seen. On special occasions, kākāpō heads were strung by the nostrils and worn in the ears. The bird was hunted for food too, both by Māori and by European gold prospectors, but was given legal protection in 1896. It is believed to have originally flown to New Zealand as a much smaller bird – perhaps no larger than a budgerigar. Generation by generation, it grew into this flightless nocturnal giant, for it had plenty of food and few predators – until humans and dogs arrived here, some 1,000 years ago. At that point, kākāpō were found throughout North, South and Stewart Islands. Nowadays, the bird is endangered, and found only in native forest on Maud and Codfish Islands – although neither of these islands are open to the public. Also known as the ground parrot or owl parrot.

◆ Green back *(unlike pūkeko)*

◆ Legs shorter &
heavier than on a
pūkeko *(page 60)*

Takahē

Porphyrio hochstetteri [Rallidae]

Native
& found only in New Zealand
Sanctuary bird (0)

3000g	63cm

◆ *Three times the size of a pūkeko
(standing almost knee-high)*
◆ Cannot fly *(unlike pūkeko)*
◆ Call similar to weka: 'coo-eet'

For fifty years the takahē was thought to be extinct – that is until its exciting rediscovery by Dr Geoffrey Orbell on 20th November, 1948. We now know that it still lives in tussock grassland and beech forest in the Murchison Mountains, west of Lake Te Anau, where it eats mainly tussock stems and starchy fern roots. To protect the remaining birds, this area is not open to the public, but takahē can easily be seen on Tiritiri Matangi and Kapiti Islands. They are also kept at Mt Bruce Wildlife Centre near Masterton and at Te Anau Wildlife Centre. Birds raised at Te Anau (Burwood Bush) are fed by using takahē glove puppets. This prevents the chicks from being confused into thinking that their parents are really people. The puppets are also used to teach the chicks the dangers of stoats; the chicks watch a stuffed stoat attacking a takahē glove puppet and soon learn to hide themselves when the stuffed stoat reappears. Many of these trained birds can then be released back into the wild. Here the main threats to their survival are red deer (which compete for takahē food) and the stoats. Otherwise, the birds are thought to be able to live to 14-20 years old. Takahē were roasted and eaten by early sealers. They were eaten by early Māori too, as was a slightly larger cousin, *Porphyrio mantelli* from the North Island, along with several similar flightless birds (**adzebill** and rails) – all now extinct. The takahē and **pūkeko** (page 60) are believed to be descended from two invasions of the same bird: the Australian purple swamphen. Whereas the ancestors of the pūkeko arrived about 1,000 years ago, the original ancestors of the takahē must have flown to New Zealand over ten million years ago. The takahē kept its wings, but, over many generations, slowly lost its ability to fly.

Mountain Birds

(Birds found above the tree-line)

Where the land is too high and cold for forest to grow, New Zealand's mountain birds are found. Some (like the rock wren) are found only here, but others (like the black-backed gull) are common at lower altitudes.

Birds found *only* in the mountains are described in detail in this section, but *all* those birds likely to be seen in the mountains are shown together in the picture key on the facing page, along with the relevant page numbers.

TIPS for Birdwatching in Mountains

◆ **North Island Mountains** have few birds: skylark, harrier, black-backed gull, redpoll, pipit (plus a few banded dotterel – page 72). The tree-line in North Island mountains is at around 1,450 metres above sea level.

◆ **South Island Mountains** have the best range of mountain birds, including all the birds on the facing page. The tree-line in South Island mountains is at around 900 metres. (Although some takahē – page 25 – are found in the Murchison Mountains, this area is closed to the public.)

◆ **Stewart Island Mountains** A surprising bird to find here is the New Zealand dotterel (page 73) which breeds above the tree-line.

KEY: Mountain Birds often Found by their Call

	page	
Rock Wren	28	Quiet, high-pitched: '**zit**, zit, zit' *(South Island only; rare)*
Skylark	41	Sings non-stop while flying
Pipit	41	Shrill: 'peepit' or 'scree'
Falcon	17	Shrill scream: '**keek-keek-keek-keek-keek**' *(South Island mountains)*
Chukor	48	A loud: 'chuk-chuk-chuk-chukar' *(South Island)*
Kea	29	Wavering screech: '**ke-e-e-e-a**' *(South Island only)*

KEY: MOUNTAIN BIRDS

The birds are placed in this picture according to where they are most likely to be seen.
They are arranged in order of size, with the smallest bird in each group at the left.

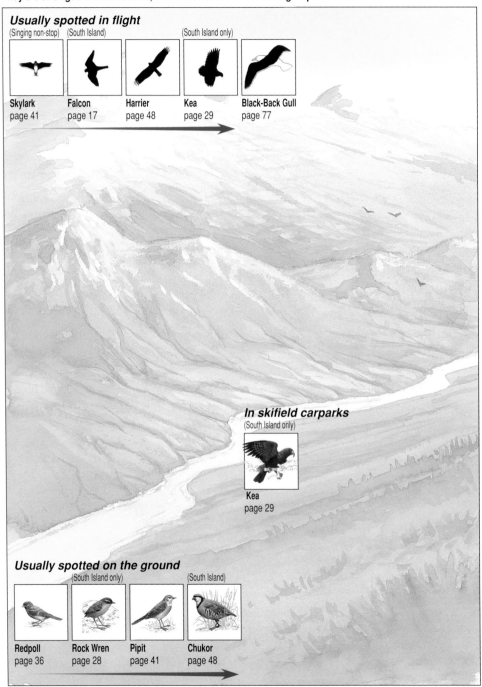

Usually spotted in flight

(Singing non-stop) (South Island)   (South Island only)

Skylark   **Falcon**   **Harrier**   **Kea**   **Black-Back Gull**
page 41   page 17   page 48   page 29   page 77

In skifield carparks
(South Island only)

Kea
page 29

Usually spotted on the ground
(South Island only)   (South Island)

Redpoll   **Rock Wren**   **Pipit**   **Chukor**
page 36   page 28   page 41   page 48

MALE
◆ Dull green back

◆ Very short tail

FEMALE
◆ Pale brown

Rock Wren / Hurupounamu

Xenicus gilviventris [Acanthisittidae]

| **Native** |
| *& found only in New Zealand* |
| Rare (1) |
| 16/20g | 10cm |

◆ **In South Island mountains only**
◆ Seen on the ground bobbing up & down or running; seldom flies
◆ Flicks its wings
◆ Call: a high-pitched '**zit**, zit, zit'
◆ *Larger than a rifleman (page 8)*

◆ Large feet with unusually long back claws

Few people will ever notice this tiny bird unless they are lucky enough to hear a mouse-like squeak coming from amongst a pile of fallen rocks in the South Island mountains. For the rock wren lives more like a mouse than a bird, feeding on (or even under) the ground, eating mainly insects and spiders. Although commonest close to the tree-line, it has been seen as high as 2,500 metres above sea level. In winter, it does not migrate to lower altitudes as one might expect, but remains in the mountains, hiding in rock crevices beneath the snow or feeding in air spaces between boulders and scrub. Only rarely does it fly. One of the easiest places to find one these days is either side of the Homer Tunnel, near Milford Sound, close to the tree-line. The rock wren was not discovered by Europeans until the 1860s, by which time it had already disappeared from the North Island. Early explorers, keen to collect the birds for museum collections, commented that they were not easily frightened when they threw stones at them or even when fired at. Perhaps because it has had so little contact with people, it is not scared to accept feathers offered to it in spring for lining its nest. (It can use as many as 800 feathers for lining just one nest.) This bulky rock-crevice nest has a circular entrance hole on one side; inside, the bird lays 1-5 eggs. The rock wren can live to at least 8 years old. The slightly smaller rifleman (page 8) is the rock wren's only other close living relative. Another close relative, the **bush wren** went by the same Māori names: hurupounamu and mātuitui. It lived at lower altitudes in forest and scrub and was last seen on Kaimohu Island (off Stewart Island) in 1972, but is now thought to be extinct. A fourth New Zealand wren (the so-called **Stephen's Island wren**) is thought to have behaved in much the same mouse-like way. It lived in the North and South Islands too, but was not discovered until 1894, when the lighthouse keeper's cat on Stephen's Island brought one home. Its owner is the only European ever to see one alive, and his cat collected the last 17 birds in existence.

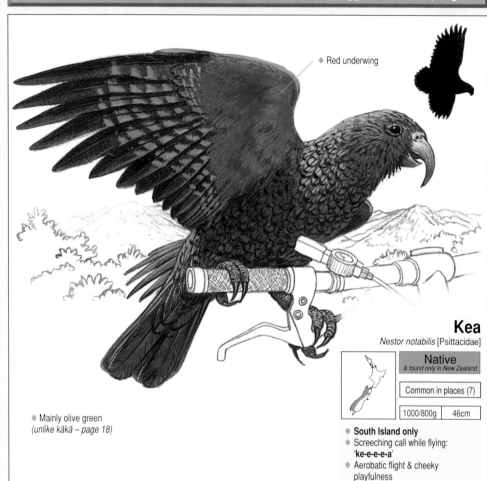

◆ Red underwing

◆ Mainly olive green
(unlike kākā – page 18)

MOUNTAIN

Kea
Nestor notabilis [Psittacidae]

Native	
& found only in New Zealand	
Common in places (7)	
1000/800g	46cm

◆ **South Island only**
◆ Screeching call while flying:
   '**ke-e-e-e-a**'
◆ Aerobatic flight & cheeky
   playfulness

Wild parrots are best-known from tropical rainforests, so it is a surprise to find one at home in the snow. Indeed, the kea is one of the world's few alpine parrots. It lives only in the South Island – mainly in the mountains – usually near the tree-line, but also among the snowy mountain tops. On the western side of the Southern Alps, it comes right down into low-lying flat country. It is often first noticed in skifields and alpine carparks. The kea eats mostly fruit, seeds, leaves and buds, but also insects, bird chicks and dead animals. Many have learnt to search through rubbish dumps in search of meat scraps and leftover dairy products. Among South Island farmers, the bird has the reputation of being a sheep killer, though attacks on healthy sheep are rare. A few individuals do, however, get a taste for sheep, and will peck at healthy animals, digging into flesh above the kidneys, proof of which has been captured on video with infra-red lights at night. Nineteenth-century claims, however, that 'run-holders have been driven off [their farms by attacks on their sheep by kea]' turned out to be entirely fabricated. Early explorers shot or stoned them for food and farmers shot them to reduce attacks on sheep. Indeed, a bounty was even paid for kea beaks by local government, and the official records show that over a 70 year period, more than 150,000 birds were killed. About 5,000 birds now remain, thanks in part to their having been given full legal protection, which they received as recently as 1986. These days, kea are probably best known for their comical habit of sliding down the roofs of tents, tramping huts or the windscreens of parked cars, or perching on the glass edge of half-open car windows. But their playfulness easily turns to destructiveness when they peck at rubber seals from windscreens, and wiper blades, tyre rims and valve stems or rip into feather sleeping bags and tents. Nuisance birds are sometimes caught and kept as caged pets. Surprisingly, they nest in burrows in high altitude forest and scrub. Although usually olive green, the occasional bright yellow bird has also been seen. The bird's Māori name comes from the sound of its screeching call. The kea can live to over 20 years old. There is no indication that kea were ever common in the North Island.

The colour art on this page is shown at: QUARTER LIFE-SIZE

Countryside & Garden Birds

(Birds of towns, parks, gardens, orchards, farmland, scrub, roads & powerlines)

These birds all live near people so are the ones most people notice.

Here, in gardens and farmland, many more species of birds can be found than in forest. Most of these birds were brought here from other countries (introduced), but a few of New Zealand's more adaptable native birds (like the fantail and pūkeko) are quite at home here too.

The beginner may not know which birds are introduced and which ones are native, so both are shown together in the picture keys in the following pages.

TIPS for Birdwatching in Countryside & Gardens

◆ The home garden is a great place to start birdwatching, so long as the garden has trees and shrubs for shelter, nesting and food. More birds will come if you also provide a bird bath and safe bird table – out of reach of cats!

◆ If you live on a farm, you may wish to make a pond with an island in it too and arrange safe perching spots for the birds nearby.

◆ Note that birds are easily disturbed by dogs, cats and people.

◆ Good birdwatching spots in open countryside include shrubby sand dunes and quiet, shrubby roadside verges.

KEY: Countryside & Garden Birds often Found by their Call

Many birds have a range of song including special calls for raising the alarm, for finding a mate or establishing territory. Only common songs or calls are listed.

In Full Song While Flying

	page		
Redpoll	36	'Chich-chich-chich' *(sometimes followed by a short rippling trill)*	*All year*
Skylark	41	Sings non-stop while hovering high overhead	*Aug-Jan*

Garden Songbirds
Continuous song or melody usually sung by the male, saying 'This is my territory!' or 'I want a mate!' Most introduced songbirds are seasonal singers. They are listed here in the order in which they are first heard. (Native songbirds – most of which sing throughout the year – are listed on page 5.)

	page		
Dunnock	38	Hurried warble: 'weeso, sissy-weeso, sissy-weeso, sissy-wee'	*April-Jan*
Thrush	42	Repeated phrases: '**Did** you do it? **Did** you do it? **I** saw you. **I** saw you..'	*May-Dec*
Chaffinch	38	'Chip chip chip tell tell tell cherry-erry-erry tissi **cheweeo**'	*July-Jan*
Blackbird	43	Loud, sweet musical song with piping notes *(with pauses, no repeats)*	*July-Jan*
Greenfinch	39	'Chichichi tu zweet zweet zweet'	*Aug-Feb*
Yellowhammer	39	'A little bit of bread and no **cheese**'	*Aug-Feb*
Shining Cuckoo	12	'Tu**wee** tu**wee** tu**wee** tu**wee** tu**wee** tiw**oo**'	*Sep-Jan*
Goldfinch	37	A jingling twitter: 'tsitt-witt-witt'	*Sep-Feb*
Starling	42	Fragile warbles, clicks, gurgles & whistles	*All year*
Myna	44	Raucous gurgling, chattering, with bell-like notes	*All year*
Magpie	46	'Quardle oodle ardle wardle doodle' *(loud)*	*All year*

Simple Daytime Calls (Not musical)

	page	
Pipit	41	Shrill: 'peepit' or 'scree'
Kingfisher	55	Loud: '**weet-weet-weet**' *(from perch)*
Rosella	44	Chattering, screeching or 'kwink' call *(from tops of trees)*
California Quail	45	'Mac**wer**ta, mac**wer**ta, mac**wer**ta' *(in scrub)*
Myna	44	'**A**chukee **a**chukee **a**chukee' *(& many other sounds – North Island)*
Spur-Winged Plover	46	Loud, gull-like: '**kitter kitter kitter**' *(on farmland)*
Pūkeko	60	Loud screech
Paradise Shelduck	62	Deep '**klonk klonk**' *(male)* answered by '**zeek zeek**' *(female)*
Pheasant	49	Very loud: 'kok **kok**' *(male)* *(in scrub – mostly North Island)*

Common Night Calls

	page	
Morepork	16	'**More pork**' repeated + '**krree**' *(from perch)*
Pied Stilt	74	Barking or yapping call *(flying overhead)*
Spur-Winged Plover	46	Loud, gull-like: '**kitter kitter kitter**' *(on farmland or flying overhead)*
Pūkeko	60	Loud screech *(flying overhead)*

KEY: BIRDS of PARKS, GARDENS & ROADS

The birds are placed in this picture according to where they are most likely to be first seen.
They are arranged in order of size, with the smallest bird in each group at the top left.

Around trees, shrubs or tall weeds

(South Island only)

Grey Warbler	Redpoll	Goldfinch	Shining Cuckoo	Bellbird	Tūi	Morepork	Little Owl
page 8	page 36	page 37	page 12	page 13	page 15	page 16	page 45

At bird bath or bird table, or on lawns

Fantail	Silvereye	Dunnock	Chaffinch
page 9	page 10	page 38	page 38

Greenfinch	Sparrow	Thrush	Starling
page 39	page 40	page 42	page 42

(North Island only)

Blackbird	Rosella	Myna
page 43	page 44	page 44

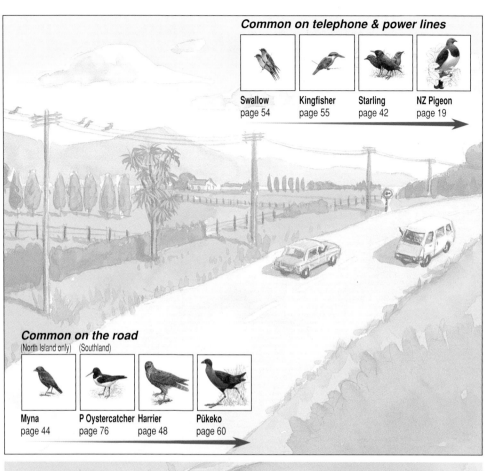

Common on telephone & power lines

Swallow
page 54

Kingfisher
page 55

Starling
page 42

NZ Pigeon
page 19

Common on the road
(North Island only) (Southland)

Myna
page 44

P Oystercatcher
page 76

Harrier
page 48

Pūkeko
page 60

Very common in parks & city streets
(Park lakes often have mallard, black swan, pūkeko and coot too – see page 52)

Chaffinch
page 38

Sparrow
page 40

Red-Bill Gull
page 75

Rock Pigeon
page 47

Black-Back Gull
page 77

KEY: FARMLAND BIRDS (For freshwater birds go to pages 51-53.)

The birds are placed in this picture according to where they are most likely to be first seen.
They are arranged in order of size, with the smallest bird in each group at the top left.

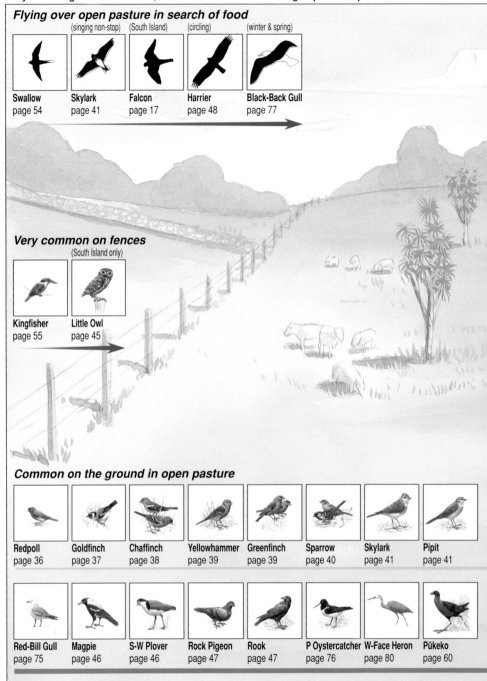

Flying over open pasture in search of food

	(singing non-stop)	(South Island)	(circling)	(winter & spring)
Swallow page 54	**Skylark** page 41	**Falcon** page 17	**Harrier** page 48	**Black-Back Gull** page 77

Very common on fences

(South Island only)

Kingfisher page 55   **Little Owl** page 45

Common on the ground in open pasture

Redpoll page 36	**Goldfinch** page 37	**Chaffinch** page 38	**Yellowhammer** page 39	**Greenfinch** page 39	**Sparrow** page 40	**Skylark** page 41	**Pipit** page 41
Red-Bill Gull page 75	**Magpie** page 46	**S-W Plover** page 46	**Rock Pigeon** page 47	**Rook** page 47	**P Oystercatcher** page 76	**W-Face Heron** page 80	**Pūkeko** page 60

Common around scrub, hedges & shelterbelts
(spring & summer)

Grey Warbler page 8	**Fantail** page 9	**Silvereye** page 10	**Dunnock** page 38	**Shining Cuckoo** page 12	**Bellbird** page 13	**Thrush** page 42

Blackbird page 43	**Tūi** page 15	**Rosella** page 44	**Morepork** page 16	**California Quail** page 45	**NZ Pigeon** page 19	**Pheasant** page 49

(spring & summer)   (North Island only)

Blk-Front Tern page 56	**Starling** page 42	**Myna** page 44	**Pied Stilt** page 74	**Black-Bill Gull** page 57

Black-Back Gull page 77	**Mallard** page 62	**Paradise Duck** page 62	**Canada Goose** page 65	**Black Swan** page 66

Grey Warbler / Riroriro
Go to page 8

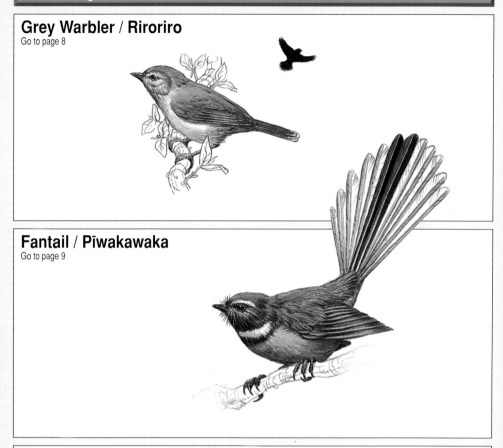

Fantail / Pīwakawaka
Go to page 9

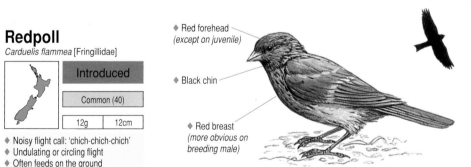

Redpoll
Carduelis flammea [Fringillidae]

Introduced	
Common (40)	
12g	12cm

- Noisy flight call: 'chich-chich-chich'
- Undulating or circling flight
- Often feeds on the ground

- ◆ Red forehead *(except on juvenile)*
- ◆ Black chin
- ◆ Red breast *(more obvious on breeding male)*

The dull colouring of this little finch means that it often goes unnoticed, yet the redpoll is common, particularly in high, dry areas of the South Island, but also throughout the country right down to sand dunes at sea level. The redpoll eats mainly weed seeds, but also some insects and fruit buds, using its powerful gizzard for breaking up seeds. It plays a useful part in attacking insect pests. In winter, it feeds in flocks of up to 250 birds or more; one flock in the King Country was estimated to have over 100,000 birds. It nests in low shrubs. Redpolls were brought here from Europe in the 1860s, but are also found naturally in North America and Asia. It is sometimes kept as a cage bird and can live to about 8 years old.

Silvereye / Tauhou
Go to page 10

Welcome Swallow / Warou
Go to page 54

Goldfinch
Carduelis carduelis [Fringillidae]

Introduced	
Very common (60)	
16/15g	13cm

◆ Bright red face *(on adults)*

◆ Bright yellow band on wings

◆ Undulating flight, showing flash of gold on wings
◆ Male song a twittering 'tsitt-witt-witt' (Sep-Feb)
◆ Males & females look the same

A beautiful and very common finch seen in farmland, orchards and gardens – sometimes on beaches too. The goldfinch eats some insects but mainly uses its powerful gizzard to break up seeds, making it a useful destroyer of weed seeds such as thistle and dandelion. It is often seen in large winter flocks of 50-500 birds, sometimes even with as many as 15,000. With the goldfinch's vibrant colours, it is not surprising that huge numbers were trapped in nineteenth-century England for the cage-bird trade. It can live to about 8 years old. The goldfinch was brought here from Europe in the 1860s, but is found naturally also in North Africa, the Middle East and western Asia.

For easy comparison, the colour art on these two pages is all to the same scale: HALF LIFE-SIZE

Dunnock (Hedge Sparrow)
Prunella modularis [Prunellidae]

Introduced	
Very common (50)	
21g	14cm

◆ Fine, pointed bill
(unlike house sparrow)

- ◆ Often feeds on bare ground, near hedges or shrubs
- ◆ Fast warbling song (April-Jan) from a high perch: 'weeso, sissy-weeso, sissy-weeso, sissy-wee' (male)
- ◆ *Slimmer than a house sparrow (page 40)*

Because of its secretive habits and drab colouring, the dunnock is not often noticed and is certainly not well known, in spite of being very common. It is sometimes called the 'hedge sparrow' because it never strays far from hedges or shrubs, and because it looks like a house sparrow (although the two birds are quite unrelated). In gardens, the dunnock can often be attracted into view with a bird bath. It eats insects, spiders and worms (with some fruit and seeds), usually taken from the ground, not far from cover. It is common, too, among sand dune lupins, along roadsides, in parks, gardens, orchards, scrub and forest, where it can sometimes get caught up in the barbed seeds of hook grass. It is useful in controlling insect pests, having largely cleared Otago orchards of aphids. It was brought here from Europe in the 1860s, but breeds also in western Asia. From both these continents, a few migrate south to the Mediterranean and North Africa. Dunnocks can live to more than six years old.

Chaffinch / Pahirini
Fringilla coelebs [Fringillidae]

Introduced	
Very common (90)	
22/21g	15cm

- ◆ Shuffles *(rather than walks or hops)*
- ◆ Undulating flight with white wingbar & outer tail feathers
- ◆ Male song from high perch (July-Jan): 'chip chip chip tell tell tell cherry-erry-erry tissi **cheweeo**'

FEMALE

MALE
◆ Pinkish brown breast
(more brightly coloured at breeding time)

There is nowhere too remote for the chaffinch. Brought here from Europe in the 1860s, this finch is now common throughout the country – in parks, gardens, farmland and scrub, even deep inside native and exotic forest, and sometimes even in the mountains, above the tree line. They feed on the ground, eating seeds, insects spiders and the small fruits of native shrubs and trees. Like other finches, they have a powerful gizzard for breaking up seeds. They are often encouraged into parks and gardens to take crumbs from bird tables and picnickers. In autumn and winter they form flocks of several hundred birds, often with all the birds in the flock being of the same sex, hence an old name for the chaffinch: 'bachelor bird'. Chaffinches have been seen picking up individual ants to rub in their flight feathers as an insecticide to control feather lice and mites. It is also found naturally in the North Atlantic islands, North Africa, the Middle East and Asia and can live for about 10 years.

Yellowhammer
Emberiza citrinella [Emberizidae]

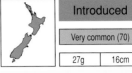

Introduced	
Very common (70)	
27g	16cm

◆ Bright yellow head, chest & underneath *(female duller)*

◆ Feeds mainly on the ground, hopping
◆ Flight often undulating, showing white outer tail feathers
◆ Male sings from perch (Aug-Feb): 'a little bit of bread and no **cheese**'

The song of this pretty yellow finch-like bird is often compared to the phrase: 'a little bit of bread and no **cheese**'; a phrase said to have inspired the opening lines of Beethoven's Fifth Symphony. Yellowhammers were brought here in the 1860s from Europe and are probably now more common here than in England. They are found mostly in rough open country and orchards from sea level to subalpine tussock, and are not common in built-up areas. In winter and spring, they can gather in large flocks of up to 200-300 birds. A century ago, large numbers were killed and eggs destroyed as yellowhammers were eating newly-sown pasture seeds and destroying haystacks, although it is doubtful now whether they were ever really a serious nuisance. The yellowhammer eats seeds, insects and spiders and builds a rough nest on, or near, the ground. Its natural range is from Britain to Siberia, with many birds migrating south from there to North Africa, the Middle East and southern Asia. In northern winters, it has been known to withstand temperatures of −36°C. It can live to about 10 years old. A less colourful relative, the **cirl bunting**, is sometimes seen in the north and east of the South Island.

MALE
◆ Olive green head & back

◆ Bright yellow along edge of wings

FEMALE

◆ Bill heavier than on other finches

Greenfinch
Carduelis chloris [Fringillidae]

Introduced	
Common (40)	
28g	15cm

◆ Undulating flight, showing yellow on tail & wings
◆ Male sings (Aug-Feb) from high perch in descending notes: 'chichichi tu zweet zweet zweet' or a jeering 'dzwee'

The greenfinch was brought here from Europe in the 1860s and is now common in larger gardens, hedged farmland, orchards and the edges of pine forest. It can be attracted into gardens with a bird table. Its main food is seeds, which it breaks up with its powerful gizzard. It eats fruit buds too and some insects, which it will happily pick out of car radiators. In winter and spring, flocks of up to 1,000 birds or more can be seen among farm weeds, with one flock numbering over 10,000 birds. Found naturally also in North Africa, the Middle East and western Asia. It is sometimes kept as a cage bird here and can live to about 10 years old.

COUNTRYSIDE & GARDEN

House Sparrow / Tiu

Passer domesticus [Ploceidae]

Introduced

Very common (75)

30g	14cm

- The most common city bird
- Feeds mainly on the ground
- Hops rather than shuffles
  (unlike chaffinch – page 38)
- Often seen taking 'dust baths'
- Flight fast & direct

FEMALE
- No black bib

- Short, cone-shaped bill *(unlike dunnock – page 38)*

MALE *(at breeding time)*
- Black bib

This bird is seen in such large numbers in towns and cities that many people would think the sparrow was New Zealand's commonest bird. But, unlike the blackbird, the sparrow is not found in forests. In the 1860s, a Mr Bills trapped hundreds of the birds in London and sent them to New Zealand to help control insect pests in crops. When the new arrivals were then attacked by kingfishers, many angry settlers called for our native kingfishers to be shot. But the sparrow survived, soon to become New Zealand's greatest bird pest for, in reality, the house sparrow eats far more seeds than insects. True, it helped control cattle ticks, but its main favourites turned out to be farmers' wheat, barley and maize, sometimes feeding in flocks of several hundred birds. In towns, it has learnt to trigger the electronic sensors of automatic sliding doors to reach café crumbs, flying into warehouses, supermarkets and hospitals too, to find human-produced food, such a bread, sugar and fat. It has discovered too that car radiators are a great source of dead insects. It is also common on beaches, especially among sand dunes and is seen taking nectar from pōhutukawa and flax flowers. It can be a nuisance where it builds nests in gutters, drainpipes and chimneys and when pulling the insulation off powerlines. It is one of the easiest birds to attract to the garden with a bird bath or with crumbs left on a bird table. At dusk, large groups are often heard chattering from nests in dense trees or hedges, particularly in bamboo or tall conifer trees. To control lice in their feathers, sparrows have been seen 'bathing' in the smoke from house chimneys. Can live to over 15 years old. The odd bird can be buff, white (albino), or with white on the wings or tail. The sparrow is found naturally in Europe, North Africa, the Middle East, Asia, and has been introduced to so many other countries that it is now found over two-thirds of the world's land surface.

Bellbird / Korimako

Go to page 13

◆ Head crest sometimes noticeable

◆ White on back edge of wings

Skylark
Alauda arvensis [Alaudidae]

Introduced	
Very common (70)	
38g	18cm

◆ Male sings non-stop while hovering high overhead *(unlike pipit – below)*
◆ Feeds on the ground

Early European settlers so missed the skylark's warbling flight song, that, in the 1860s, they brought this bird to New Zealand. And now, the skylark is far more common here than in England. It is usually noticed in spring, singing non-stop while hovering high overhead, sometimes for as long as 20 minutes at a stretch. It sings while rising almost vertically until it is almost out of sight, and just keeps on singing as it drops back down to the ground. It is very common in open country from coastal sand dunes and farmland to subalpine tussock, nesting and feeding on the ground, eating mainly seeds, with some insects and spiders. It will also eat young vegetable plants and sown grain, but this damage is far outweighed by the good it does in controlling insect pests. To wash, it lies down in the rain with both wings extended or takes dust baths along the edge of gravel roads. It is such a symbol of wide, open spaces, that it is hard to believe that it is sometimes kept as a cage bird. The skylark is also found naturally in North Africa, the Middle East and Asia. It can live to about 8 years old.

◆ No crest *(unlike skylark)*
◆ Clear white eyebrow

◆ Bill longer & finer than skylark *(above)*

NZ Pipit / Pīhoihoi
Anthus novaeseelandiae [Motacillidae]

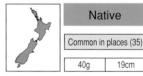

Native	
Common in places (35)	
40g	19cm

◆ Often runs a short distance & stops, flicking its tail *(unlike skylark)*
◆ Makes short, fast swoops *(unlike skylark – above)*
◆ Calls from low perch: 'pi-pit'
◆ Feeds mostly on the ground

The pipit is probably best known from sandy beaches, where it has the odd habit of running and stopping (often coming quite close), then flicking its tail up and down. But this bird is also found hopping up coastal cliffs, in rough pasture, along shingle riverbeds, gravel roads and scrubby roadsides and way up into the mountains too, right above the tree-line. Pipits eat mainly insects, spiders and sandhoppers, but also some seeds, feeding mostly on the ground. To the farmer, they are useful in controlling grass grubs and cattle ticks. They build their nest on the ground. When returning to it, they fly to a spot nearby and walk the last 5-10 metres. Although found naturally in many other countries (where it is known as Richard's pipit), the four subspecies seen here are found only in New Zealand, with three of these seen only on offshore islands. Because of its habit of staying close to the ground, and the fact that it is so easily confused with the skylark, it used to be called the ground lark, but larks and pipits are not closely related.

Song Thrush
Turdus philomelos [Muscicapidae]

Introduced	
Very common (75)	
70g	23cm

◆ Dark brown spots on breast

◆ White belly

- ◆ Feeds mostly on the ground (hopping)
- ◆ Male sings from high perch, repeated phrases: 'Did you do it? Did you do it? I saw you. I saw you...' (May-Dec)
- ◆ Males & females look the same

The song thrush runs or hops a few steps, then stops with its head cocked, apparently listening for worms to pull from the ground. But the bird is not listening; it is simply tilting its head to get a better view. When eating snails, it often carries them to a special stone on which to smash the shells open. Such thrush anvil stones can often be seen with a pile of twenty or more broken shells scattered nearby. But, apart from eating common garden snails, it also eats rare native land snails, insects, spiders, millipedes, hoppers and some fruit. It is sometimes seen squatting with its wings spread among ants, encouraging the insects to release formic acid into its feathers as an insecticide. Thrushes are very common in gardens, parks, orchards, farm hedges, forests and scrub right up to subalpine altitudes. A bird bath will attract them into the garden. Sometimes kept as a cage bird, this thrush is found naturally in Europe and Asia and was brought to New Zealand in the 1860s for its song. It can live to over 10 years old. The similar-looking, but quite unrelated **New Zealand thrush** (**piopio**) was a member of Australian bowerbird family. It has been extinct since about 1902.

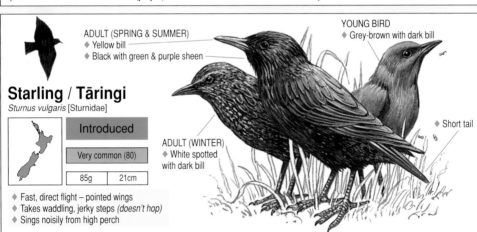

ADULT (SPRING & SUMMER)
- ◆ Yellow bill
- ◆ Black with green & purple sheen

YOUNG BIRD
- ◆ Grey-brown with dark bill

Starling / Tāringi
Sturnus vulgaris [Sturnidae]

Introduced	
Very common (80)	
85g	21cm

ADULT (WINTER)
- ◆ White spotted with dark bill

◆ Short tail

- ◆ Fast, direct flight – pointed wings
- ◆ Takes waddling, jerky steps *(doesn't hop)*
- ◆ Sings noisily from high perch

The starling imitates the calls of other birds, copying police sirens, ringing telephones and traffic noise too. One starling at a cage bird show in Vienna had a clear vocabulary of seventy words. It is one of the most common birds in open farmland, orchards and gardens, along roadsides, sitting on powerlines, in the edges of forests, on beaches, nesting in holes in trees, buildings and cliffs. It jabs its bill into the ground for grubs and worms or catches flying insects on the wing. It also eats snails and spiders, fruit and nectar. In spring, when visiting pōhutukawa and flax flowers, its head is often covered with orange-red pollen. Farmers, appreciating starlings for the control of grass grubs and cattle ticks, sometimes build starling boxes on high fence posts as safe nesting places inaccessible to mynas. These boxes helped compensate for a loss of starlings during the 1940s, due apparently to the effects of using DDT pesticide. On the down side, the starling competes for food with bellbird, tūī and kererū, and can destroy the nests of native birds. In winter, they are seen feeding in large, noisy flocks of up to 1,000 birds, sometimes gathering into even larger flocks of over 1,000,000 birds, making them a danger to aircraft. (The birds see it the other way round.) In late summer, starlings will pick up a billful of worker ants to rub in their wing feathers to control lice and mites, or bathe in the smoke from chimneys for the same reason. Starlings were brought here from Europe in the 1860s to control insect pests in farmland and are now common in many parts of the world. They can live for about 20 years.

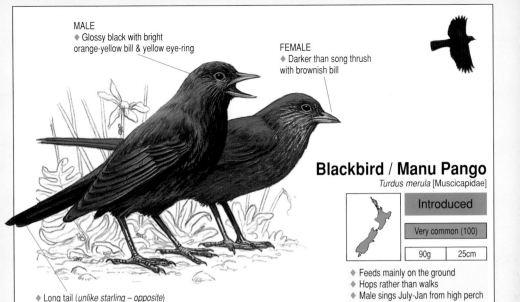

MALE
◆ Glossy black with bright orange-yellow bill & yellow eye-ring

FEMALE
◆ Darker than song thrush with brownish bill

Blackbird / Manu Pango
Turdus merula [Muscicapidae]

Introduced
Very common (100)

90g	25cm

◆ Feeds mainly on the ground
◆ Hops rather than walks
◆ Male sings July-Jan from high perch
(song not repeated like song thrush)

◆ Long tail *(unlike starling – opposite)*

COUNTRYSIDE & GARDEN

This is New Zealand's most common bird, for the blackbird is found not only in gardens, parks, orchards, around farm hedges and in scrub, but also deep inside mature forests. In forest, it is much more shy and not easily noticed except for its alarm call as it takes off from the ground: 'tok tok tok tok'. Here, it competes for food with native berry-eating birds and with native insect-eaters such as the New Zealand robin, as it searches the leaf litter for insects – either scratching the ground with its feet or using its bill to flick aside the leaves. It also eats native skinks and attacks native birds. In the countryside, it damages orchard fruit and spreads weed seeds, but is useful in helping to control grass grubs. The blackbird is sometimes kept as a cage bird and is easily attracted to the garden with a bird bath or with meat scraps or pieces of apple on a bird table. Like its relative, the song thrush, it is often seen taking a few hops and stopping with its head cocked, seeming to listen for worms to pull from the ground. It has the comic habit of crouching on the ground with its wings spread to sunbathe, or sitting in a half squat position among ants with its wings spread, stimulating these insects to squirt formic acid into its feathers as an insecticide to control mites and lice. Sometimes, it will pick up the ants and place them under its wing feathers. It is not unusual to see it attacking its own reflection in a window. In spite of its name, the odd blackbird can be completely white (albino) or – more commonly – black and white (part albino). It was brought here from Europe in the 1860s, but is found naturally also in north western Africa, the Middle East and Asia. Blackbirds can live for about 20 years.

Tūī
Go to page 15

◆ Pair of white throat tufts on adult bird *(unlike blackbird – above)*

For easy comparison, the colour art on these two pages is all to the same scale: THIRD LIFE-SIZE

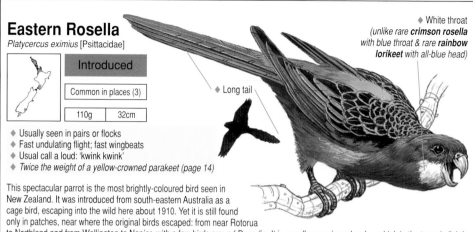

Eastern Rosella
Platycercus eximius [Psittacidae]

Introduced	
Common in places (3)	
110g	32cm

- Usually seen in pairs or flocks
- Fast undulating flight; fast wingbeats
- Usual call a loud: 'kwink kwink'
- *Twice the weight of a yellow-crowned parakeet (page 14)*

♦ Long tail

♦ White throat
(unlike rare **crimson rosella** with blue throat & rare **rainbow lorikeet** with all-blue head)

This spectacular parrot is the most brightly-coloured bird seen in New Zealand. It was introduced from south-eastern Australia as a cage bird, escaping into the wild here about 1910. Yet it is still found only in patches, near where the original birds escaped: from near Rotorua to Northland and from Wellington to Napier, with a few birds around Dunedin. It is usually seen in orchards, or high in the trees in lightly wooded country, but sometimes also in dense native forest, where it can break up kauri cones to eat the seeds. It can be a minor nuisance in orchards and is common in pine forest, gums (*Eucalyptus*) and scattered tōtara. It comes into parks and gardens too, where it will feed on the ground. They can be attracted by a bird bath or with a piece of apple attached to a bird table. The rosella eats seeds, fruit, flowers, buds, shoots and some insects. In native forest, it can compete with native birds, both for food and for nest sites, as it nests in holes in trees. In Australia, it will even nest in old fence posts and even rabbit holes. Other pet parrots have escaped too but these are (so far) much less common: **sulphur-crested cockatoo**, **galah**, **crimson rosella** and **rainbow lorikeet**.

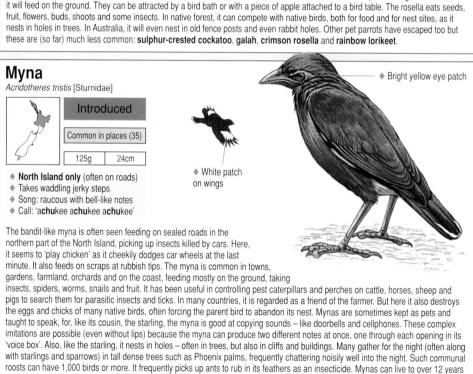

Myna
Acridotheres tristis [Sturnidae]

Introduced	
Common in places (35)	
125g	24cm

- **North Island only** (often on roads)
- Takes waddling jerky steps
- Song: raucous with bell-like notes
- Call: 'a**chu**kee a**chu**kee a**chu**kee'

♦ Bright yellow eye patch

♦ White patch on wings

The bandit-like myna is often seen feeding on sealed roads in the northern part of the North Island, picking up insects killed by cars. Here, it seems to 'play chicken' as it cheekily dodges car wheels at the last minute. It also feeds on scraps at rubbish tips. The myna is common in towns, gardens, farmland, orchards and on the coast, feeding mostly on the ground, taking insects, spiders, worms, snails and fruit. It has been useful in controlling pest caterpillars and perches on cattle, horses, sheep and pigs to search them for parasitic insects and ticks. In many countries, it is regarded as a friend of the farmer. But here it also destroys the eggs and chicks of many native birds, often forcing the parent bird to abandon its nest. Mynas are sometimes kept as pets and taught to speak, for, like its cousin, the starling, the myna is good at copying sounds – like doorbells and cellphones. These complex imitations are possible (even without lips) because the myna can produce two different notes at once, one through each opening in its 'voice box'. Also, like the starling, it nests in holes – often in trees, but also in cliffs and buildings. Many gather for the night (often along with starlings and sparrows) in tall dense trees such as Phoenix palms, frequently chattering noisily well into the night. Such communal roosts can have 1,000 birds or more. It frequently picks up ants to rub in its feathers as an insecticide. Mynas can live to over 12 years old. Also known as Indian myna, for it is originally from Afghanistan and India. However, mynas are now found throughout Asia, much of the Pacific, South Africa and Australia as well. They were introduced to New Zealand in the 1870s, first of all to the South Island where they have since died out. With them came two species of ticks which were subsequently found on the now-extinct **huia**. These ticks could easily have transmitted a disease to the huia, which may have contributed to that bird's extinction in about 1920.

Little Owl
Athene noctua [Strigidae]

Introduced	
Common in places (1)	
180g	23cm

◆ **South Island only** (mostly east coast)
◆ The only owl hunting by day
◆ Flight silent & 'bouncing'
◆ Call: a high-pitched 'kiew'

◆ *Shorter tail than morepork*

◆ Brown band across throat (*unlike morepork – page 16*)

In 1906, when introduced sparrows and finches began causing a problem on Otago orchards, this owl was brought in from Germany to help. But the little owl's main food is insects, spiders and earthworms. Along roadsides, it also hunts mice, rabbits, frogs and lizards – both by day and by night – often walking on the ground or running after its food. It lives in hedges, hay barns and clumps of trees – but only in the South Island. Unlike the native morepork, it can often be seen perching in the open in late afternoon, sunning itself on a fencepost. When scared, it bobs up and down, or flies to a wire or branch, often remaining in full view. It can live to the age of 10. It is also known as the German owl, but is found naturally in other parts of Europe too, in northern Africa and western Asia. (The **barn owl** of Australia and the Solomon Islands has been seen in New Zealand too, but very rarely – about one bird every ten years or so.)

◆ Black topknot *(larger on male)*

California Quail
Callipepla californica [Phasianidae]

Introduced	
Common (20)	
180g	25cm

◆ Male call: 'mac**wer**ta, mac**wer**ta'
◆ Birds run & take off with loud whirr of wings & loud call: '**tek tek tek**'
◆ Will sometimes perch in trees too

California's official state bird was introduced from the western United States in the 1860s, and is now common here in open country with low scrub, feeding along roadsides and riverbeds. It feeds on fallen seeds, leaves and a few small insects, but runs or flies for cover when disturbed. It nests in well-hidden spots on the ground, laying up to 22 eggs at a time, many of which get eaten by hedgehogs. In autumn, the large families sometimes join up to make even larger groups of up to fifty birds. They can live for more than 11 years. The smaller Australian **brown quail** (with no topknot) is common in Northland. New Zealand's only **native quail** (**koreke**) – a very close relative of the Australian stubble quail – became extinct about 1875.

For easy comparison, the colour art on these two pages is all to the same scale: THIRD LIFE-SIZE

Australian Magpie / Makipae

Gymnorhina tibicen [Cracticidae]

Introduced	
Very common (60)	
350g	41cm

◆ Back white or black (depending on subspecies)

◆ Loud, flute-like song: 'quardle oodle ardle wardle doodle' (all year)
◆ Direct flight; rapid wingbeats

Introduced from Australia in the 1860s to help control insect pests in farmland, which it certainly does. But the magpie can be fiercely territorial, attacking many native birds too, including birds as large as heron, falcon and harrier. Until 1951, it was protected but, because of its impact on native birds, is now often trapped. It will even dive bomb people and other large animals coming near its nest, swooping from behind and sometimes striking with its claws. (If attacked, hold a twiggy branch over your head for protection, wear a hat or take a different route.) The magpie's food includes seeds, spiders, worms, snails, lizards, mice, and dead or dying sheep. It is very common in open farmland with pine, macrocarpa, willow or gum trees, but also along roadsides and in cities, sometimes even in mature forest. It usually builds its nests in trees, often using strange materials like pieces of barbed wire, string, old spoons, glass and pieces of china. Electrocuted magpies falling from power lines, with feathers alight, have been blamed for starting fires. They are sometimes kept as pets, some of which have been taught to talk, whistle tunes, or copy fire engine sirens. The magpie can live for almost 20 years. In spite of its name, it is not a close relative of the European magpie but is named for the similarity of its colouring. There are two subspecies in New Zealand: the white-backed magpie and the less common black-backed one. These interbreed.

Spur-Winged Plover

Vanellus miles [Charadriidae]

Native	
Common (20)	
370/350g	38cm

◆ Wings & tail black-tipped

◆ Call: '**kitter kitter kitter**' (day or night)
◆ Runs & stops when feeding
◆ In flight: slow wingbeats

◆ Bright yellow bill & face mask

◆ Yellow spur on wing (used as a weapon)

Pronounced 'pluvver'. Odd birds arrived here from Australia in the 1800s, but began breeding here for the first time in Invercargill in 1932. They have since spread throughout New Zealand, but remain more common in the South Island. Having made this journey without human help, it is regarded as native to New Zealand (or 'self-introduced'). The spur-winged plover is found mainly in farmland but also on estuaries, along sandy or shingle riverbeds and beaches. It helps farmers by eating grass grubs and harmful caterpillars, but also eats earthworms, seeds and leaves. In autumn and winter they can gather in flocks of up to 600 birds. At this time, groups of 5 or 6 birds can be seen strutting in rows, forwards, backwards or in circles. This is their equivalent of a 'barn dance' at which they choose a mate or where couples express their commitment to one another. They nest on the ground, defending their nests and chicks from harriers and magpies by screaming and dive-bombing them, striking these birds with their wings or sharp wing-spurs. They will chase people away from their nests too; if necessary, attacking with their wing-spurs which are long enough (over 1 cm) to penetrate clothing. They can live for over 16 years. Known in Australia as masked lapwings.

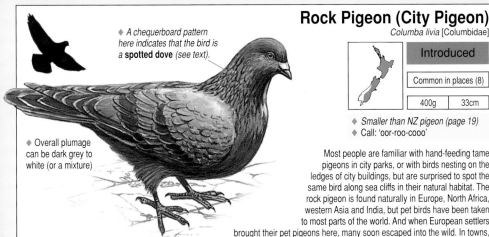

Rock Pigeon (City Pigeon)
Columba livia [Columbidae]

◆ *A chequerboard pattern here indicates that the bird is a* **spotted dove** *(see text).*

◆ Overall plumage can be dark grey to white (or a mixture)

Introduced
Common in places (8)

400g	33cm

◆ *Smaller than NZ pigeon (page 19)*
◆ Call: 'oor-roo-cooo'

Most people are familiar with hand-feeding tame pigeons in city parks, or with birds nesting on the ledges of city buildings, but are surprised to spot the same bird along sea cliffs in their natural habitat. The rock pigeon is found naturally in Europe, North Africa, western Asia and India, but pet birds have been taken to most parts of the world. And when European settlers brought their pet pigeons here, many soon escaped into the wild. In towns, they eat mainly food scraps, but in country areas they can be a nuisance in newly sown pea and bean crops. Nesting materials can include pieces of wire and nails. The chicks are fed at first on a regurgitated cheesy substance called 'pigeon milk' which comes from inside the throat of its parents. Also known as feral pigeon. City birds can be any shade from white to dark grey (or a mixture of these colours), as wild birds interbreed with newly-escaped dovecote and racing pigeons. Two related, escaped cage birds – the pale brown **spotted dove** of Asia (with chequerboard spots on its neck) and the rarer cream-coloured **Barbary dove** (from north Africa and the Middle East) – are both occasionally seen or heard in Auckland gardens.

◆ All black with grey, featherless cheeks *(unlike magpie – opposite)*

Rook
Corvus frugilegus [Corvidae]

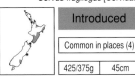

Introduced
Common in places (4)

425/375g	45cm

◆ *Bigger than Australian magpie (opposite)*
◆ Feeds on the ground
◆ Calls: 'caw', 'kah' or 'kiow'
◆ In flight: broad 'fingered' wingtips

The rook is common only in farmland around Hawke's Bay and on Banks Peninsula, near Christchurch, where it nests in the tops of tall pine trees, macrocarpas and gums. It was brought here from England in the 1860s to help control insect pests such as grass grubs. Unfortunately for farmers, it also feeds on newly sown seed, often working its way along a row, pulling them all out, one by one. Shooting and poisoning in Hawke's Bay in the 1960s and 1970s did reduce their numbers but also displaced many birds so that the rook population is now spread over a larger area. They nest in colonies of 20-100 pairs (sometimes even 900 pairs). In winter, they gather into larger flocks of up to 5,000 birds to roost. They can live to almost 20 years old. Overseas, rooks have been seen 'bathing' in smoke to control lice in their feathers. For this, they have even been known to carry smouldering twigs from bonfires to the eaves of houses, accidentally starting house fires. Rooks are found naturally from Europe and Asia, east to Siberia and Mongolia, and are sometimes kept as a cage bird. A smaller relative, the **New Zealand crow** – formerly eaten by Māori – is now extinct.

COUNTRYSIDE & GARDEN

For easy comparison, the colour art on these two pages is all to the same scale: QUARTER LIFE-SIZE

Chukor

Alectoris chukar [Phasianidae]

Introduced	
Common in places (1)	
600/500g	31cm

- **Mostly in South Island hill country**
- Call: a loud 'chuk-chuk-chuk-chukar'
- Rarely flies far

♦ Black frame around white throat & chin

This Indian partridge is found mainly on the dry, rocky hillsides of the South Island, east of the Southern Alps, especially in Otago. Although it can survive snow, the chukor usually moves to lower altitudes in winter. It is at home in the southern Himalayas of India and Nepal, but is also native to a wide band from south-eastern Europe and Turkey through to Mongolia and China. It was brought to New Zealand for sport in the 1920s and 1930s. The chukor eats mainly seeds, shoots and leaves, and swallows small stones and pebbles to help it grind tough food. It nests on the ground and stays in family groups of 5-10 birds until winter, when it gathers into larger groups of 50-150. Also called chukar – both names derived from the bird's call. It can live for over 12 years.

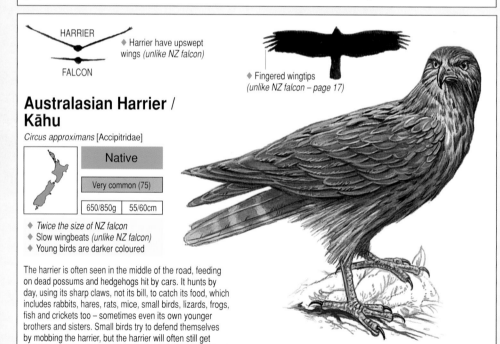

HARRIER

♦ Harrier have upswept wings *(unlike NZ falcon)*

FALCON

♦ Fingered wingtips *(unlike NZ falcon – page 17)*

Australasian Harrier / Kāhu

Circus approximans [Accipitridae]

Native	
Very common (75)	
650/850g	55/60cm

- *Twice the size of NZ falcon*
- Slow wingbeats *(unlike NZ falcon)*
- *Young birds are darker coloured*

The harrier is often seen in the middle of the road, feeding on dead possums and hedgehogs hit by cars. It hunts by day, using its sharp claws, not its bill, to catch its food, which includes rabbits, hares, rats, mice, small birds, lizards, frogs, fish and crickets too – sometimes even its own younger brothers and sisters. Small birds try to defend themselves by mobbing the harrier, but the harrier will often still get its kill. In winter and spring, it eats dead sheep and sick lambs, so early settlers poisoned the birds. Again, in the 1930s and 1940s, they were seen attacking gamebirds, so hundreds of thousands of birds were shot. Harrier did not receive legal protection until 1985. In open country, the harrier is often seen circling for hours over farmland, scrub, swamps, riverbeds or sand dunes. It is sometimes seen over forest too. From August to October, pairs can be seen doing their 'sky dance' – a spectacular courtship display of U-shaped dives. Pairs usually nest in swamps. In winter they gather here in groups of up to 150 or more. They can live to be 18 years old. Before Māori began clearing the forest, few harriers are thought to have lived in New Zealand; they were caught by Māori with baited flax snares for food and for their feathers which were used to decorate battle axes. Known also as harrier hawk or swamp harrier, it is found in Australia too, New Guinea and several Pacific Islands. The much larger **Eyles' harrier** was also eaten by Māori. It was three times this size and now extinct.

48

Very long, barred tail

FEMALE

MALE
◆ Red
eye-mask

Pheasant / Peihana
Phasianus colchicus [Phasianidae]

Introduced
Quite common (15)

1400/1200g	80/60cm

◆ Bursts noisily into flight with whirring wingbeats, then glides to the ground
◆ Very loud male call: 'kok **kok**'
◆ Seen mostly in the North Island

Since the bird's introduction to New Zealand in the 1840s, pheasant feathers have been widely used in Māori cloak-making, the plumes being inserted in rows into woven flax. This bird is found naturally from Turkey to China and was brought to North America, Europe and New Zealand for sport. Pheasants are now common in the north and west of the North Island, along back country roadsides, scrubby edges of farmland, riverbanks and in sand dunes. They find the sand useful to bathe in and use hedges, or corridors of scrub, as cover when travelling from one area to another. Pheasants feed on the ground, eating leaves, seeds, berries and insects, swallowing little sharp pebbles to help grind hard seeds in their gizzard. They nest on the ground too, making a simple scrape lined with dry grass. They often nest in hayfields but about three-quarters of these nests are destroyed by farmers when the hay is cut. Of those birds which survive, more than one third of the males are shot each year for sport. Yet populations still thrive as more birds are bred in captivity and released. They can live for over 15 years. The male often has several wives. Also known as the ring-necked pheasant. The related **wild turkey** is common in some places too, but the **peafowl** and **partridge** are much rarer in New Zealand.

Freshwater Birds

(Birds of lakes, wetlands, rivers & shingle riverbeds)

Most of our freshwater birds are native to New Zealand with several of these not being found in any other country (endemic). Besides these, a few have been introduced from overseas for sport or ornament.

The birds found in these freshwater habitats (including those more common on the coast) are all shown together in the picture keys on the following pages, with page numbers to guide you to an illustration and further information on the bird.

TIPS for Birdwatching at Rivers, Lakes and Swamps

◆ Most lake birds seek areas sheltered from the wind and prefer shallow water or shallow edges of deep water, with a safe place nearby to escape from predators. Deep lakes don't have a wide range of birds.

◆ Approach the birds quietly, as they are easily scared. If one bird raises the alarm, all the birds are likely to take off together.

◆ Check out sites marked in blue on the birdwatching hot spots map on page 92.

KEY: Freshwater Birds often Found by their Call
(Secretive birds, or those which call at night)

	page	
Fernbird	54	'Utik utik utik' (bird hidden in swamp-side scrub)
Kingfisher	55	Loud: 'weet-weet-weet-weet' (from perch)
Spotless Crake	55	Rolling: 'purrrrrrrr' (like a fast sewing machine – mostly North Island)
Banded Rail	56	'Swit swit swit' or 'craaak' (like a rusty gate opening – mostly North Island)
Pūkeko	60	Loud screech (day or night)
Bittern	64	'Boooom' (like a ship's foghorn – evenings & early mornings June to Feb)
Black Swan	66	Loud bugling (day or night)

KEY: BIRDS of FARM RIVERS
Birds are arranged in order of size, with the smallest bird in each group at the left.

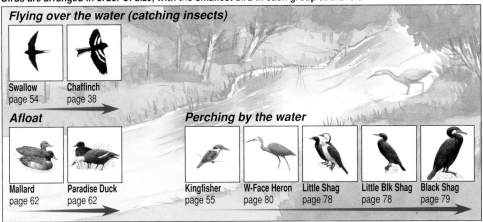

Flying over the water (catching insects)

Swallow
page 54

Chaffinch
page 38

Afloat

Mallard
page 62

Paradise Duck
page 62

Perching by the water

Kingfisher
page 55

W-Face Heron
page 80

Little Shag
page 78

Little Blk Shag
page 78

Black Shag
page 79

KEY: BIRDS of FOREST RIVERS

Perching by the water

Kingfisher
page 55

Black Shag
page 79

Afloat

Blue Duck
page 60

Grey Duck
page 61

Flying over the water (catching insects)

Swallow
page 54

Chaffinch
page 38

KEY: BIRDS of SHINGLE RIVERBEDS

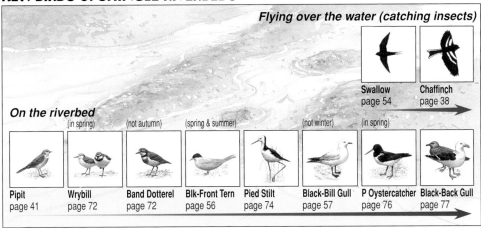

Flying over the water (catching insects)

Swallow
page 54

Chaffinch
page 38

On the riverbed

(in spring)

(not autumn)

(spring & summer)

(not winter)

(in spring)

Pipit
page 41

Wrybill
page 72

Band Dotterel
page 72

Blk-Front Tern
page 56

Pied Stilt
page 74

Black-Bill Gull
page 57

P Oystercatcher
page 76

Black-Back Gull
page 77

KEY: BIRDS of LAKES & SWAMPS

The birds are placed in this picture according to where they are most likely to be first seen.
They are arranged in order of size, with the smallest bird in each group at the left.

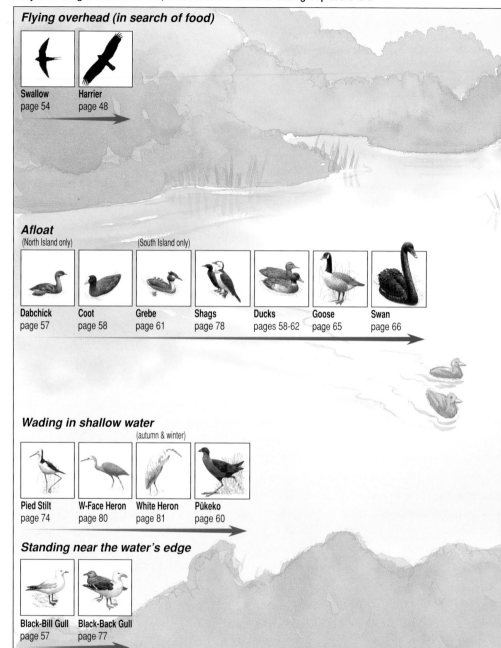

Flying overhead (in search of food)

Swallow	Harrier
page 54	page 48

Afloat

(North Island only)   (South Island only)

Dabchick	Coot	Grebe	Shags	Ducks	Goose	Swan
page 57	page 58	page 61	page 78	pages 58-62	page 65	page 66

Wading in shallow water

(autumn & winter)

Pied Stilt	W-Face Heron	White Heron	Pūkeko
page 74	page 80	page 81	page 60

Standing near the water's edge

Black-Bill Gull	Black-Back Gull
page 57	page 77

52

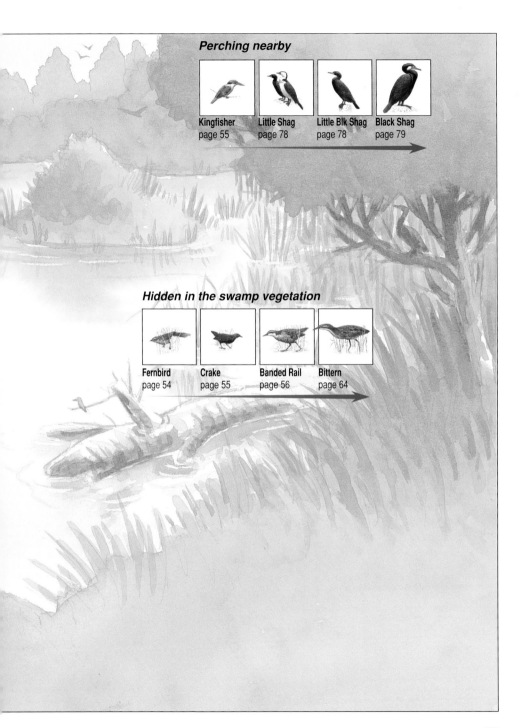

Perching nearby

Kingfisher
page 55

Little Shag
page 78

Little Blk Shag
page 78

Black Shag
page 79

Hidden in the swamp vegetation

Fernbird
page 54

Crake
page 55

Banded Rail
page 56

Bittern
page 64

53

Welcome Swallow / Warou

Hirundo tahitica [Hirundinidae]

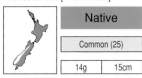

Native	
Common (25)	
14g	15cm

- ◆ Fast, flitting flight (like a bat)
- ◆ Often seen perching on wires, looking like large clothes pegs

◆ Sleek with pointed wings

◆ Deeply forked tail

The first swallow spotted in New Zealand was seen in 1920, having flown across the Tasman Sea from Australia. But it was not until 1958 that swallows started to breed here – in the Far North. The welcome swallow is found also from India to Malaysia and in the western Pacific. In New Zealand, they are common over farmland, wetlands, estuaries and mudflats, more commonly in the North Island, but continuing to spread south. They snatch small insects flying over open water, or scoop insects from the water surface. They usually fly with the stunning precision of bats, but have still been known to smack into one another in mid-air. Neat nests of mud and saliva, lined with feathers or wool, are glued onto beams beneath bridges, inside culvert pipes or on cliffs, under the eaves of buildings or in cowsheds. To keep the birds from nesting on moored yachts, boats sometimes need to be 'swallow-proofed' with plastic sheets. In autumn and winter, the birds gather near water in flocks of up to 500 birds or more. Many migrate to more northern or coastal parts of New Zealand with some regularly travelling as far afield as Norfolk Island, about 1,000 km to the north west. They can live to six years old. The only similar-looking birds in New Zealand are tropical **swifts** and Australian **martins** – both of which are exceedingly rare visitors unlikely to be seen by the beginner.

Fernbird / Mātātā

Bowdleria punctata [Sylviidae]

Native & found only in New Zealand	
Common in places (6)	
35g	18cm

- ◆ Heard more often than seen
- ◆ Call: '**utik**' (usually heard in spring)
- ◆ Slips between low branches like a mouse
- ◆ Rarely flies far

◆ Chest spotted or streaked

◆ Long frayed tail (often hanging down)

The elusive fernbird stays well-hidden in low scrub, usually near freshwater and tidal swamps (although some birds are found in low scrub and bracken well away from water, too). This bird slips through the low tangle of branches like a mouse, searching for insects and spiders or just peering out – often near head height – to check out an intruder. Before so many wetlands were drained for farming, the fernbird was much more common. Farmers can help by protecting wetland scrub from fires. One good place to see these birds bears the same name: Mātātā Lagoons, west of Whakatane. The trick to finding them is to listen for their main call: '**utik**'. This sound is usually produced by a pair of birds, one calling the '**uu**' part, the other answering: '**tik**'. Fernbirds can be easily attracted to within two metres by making simple squeaks, either by rubbing a piece of cork or polystyrene on wet glass, or simply by sucking air between your teeth. Māori saw this as a wise bird, its various calls indicating good or bad luck, depending on the call. Early settlers called it the swamp-sparrow. It can live to six years old and carries its own species of flea, known appropriately as the fernbird flea. The five subspecies of fernbird are found only in New Zealand: one each for the North Island, South Island, Stewart Island, Codfish Island and Snares Islands. The Chatham Islands had a different species of their own: a much larger bird which became extinct in about 1900.

◆ Almost black, with chocolate brown back

◆ Red eye

Spotless Crake / Pūweto
Porzana tabuensis [Rallidae]

Native	
Common in places (2)	
45g	20cm

- ◆ Mostly in the North Island, usually in raupō & reed swamps
- ◆ More often heard than seen, calling: 'purrrrrrr' (like a fast sewing machine) or pit-pit

Spotless crake are hard to see as they run and hide among raupō and reeds in swamps. Although sometimes heard at dawn and dusk, few people have seen one, except perhaps for duck-shooters or those who have had their cat bring a dead one home. It can be attracted with a tape of its purring call, which has been described as being 'like a sewing machine at high speed'; 'like a small chainsaw failing to start'; or 'like an old-fashioned alarm clock running down'. It eats worms, spiders, insects, snails, seeds and fallen fruits. On some smaller, predator-free islands, such as Tiritiri Matangi Island, it feeds quite boldly in leaf litter on the open forest floor. One bird (with an identification band attached to its leg) was moved 25 km then released, and found its way home in just six weeks. At night, they are thought to fly long distances, helping to explain why the same bird is found in several countries for, while a native of New Zealand, the spotless crake is found also in Australia, and from the Philippines and New Guinea to as far east as the Marquesas Islands. The rarer **marsh crake** looks like a small banded rail (page 56) and is more common in the South Island.

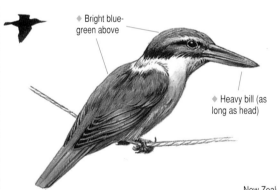

◆ Bright blue-green above

◆ Heavy bill (as long as head)

Kingfisher / Kōtare
Todiramphus sanctus (was *Halcyon sancta*) [Alcedinidae]

Native	
Very common (50)	
65g	24cm

- ◆ Often seen perching on wires, branches, rocks or fenceposts
- ◆ Call: a loud '**weet-weet-weet-weet**'
- ◆ Direct flight

New Zealand's only native kingfisher is more common in the North Island. It is often seen along the shores of estuaries, but also in farmland, near rivers or lakes, sometimes on sandy beaches along the high tide line or on rocky shores. It is common in forest too, where it is often heard but usually too high in the trees to be seen. In winter, it moves down to the coast, where it is more easily noticed, often perching on a look-out post, branch, rock or wire. From here, it dives for its prey without landing. The kingfisher hunts small crabs, large insects, spiders, earthworms, lizards, mice, tadpoles, small fish, freshwater crayfish and small birds (especially silvereyes). Its nest is a small tunnel in a clay bank or a hole in a rotting tree. It starts this tunnel by flying into the bank or tree from a distance, ramming the earth or rotten wood with its bill outstretched. It keeps this up until the hole is large enough for it to stand in. From here, it can then peck and scoop out the rest of the tunnel, which can eventually be over 30 cm long. Māori rarely ate kingfishers, for the lizards they eat represent death. This may also explain why the birds' beautiful blue feathers were not generally used to decorate clothing. Other subspecies of this kingfisher are native to Australia and New Caledonia. Australians know it as the sacred kingfisher to distinguish it from their many other kingfishers. The maniacal laughter of its noisy Australian cousin, the **kookaburra**, is sometimes heard in the Warkworth area, north of Auckland.

FRESHWATER

Black-Fronted Tern / Tarapiroe

Sterna albostriata [Laridae]

♦ Black cap meets bill
(*unlike white-fronted tern*)
(*young birds have a black-spotted cap*)

♦ Forked tail
(*unlike gulls*)

Native
& found only in New Zealand

Common in places (8)

80g	29cm

♦ *Half the weight of a white-fronted tern (page 74)*
♦ *Only inland tern of the South Island*
♦ *Often hovers with fast wingbeats*

♦ Bright orange bill (*unlike white-fronted tern*)

In spring and summer, the black-fronted tern nests on sand or shingle, along the wide, braided riverbeds of Canterbury, forming small colonies of up to 40-50 pairs. In autumn and winter, these birds move to Cook Strait and the east coast, with a few migrating as

♦ Short, bright orange legs (*unlike white-fronted tern*)

far north as the Bay of Plenty. The black-fronted tern feeds in flocks over rivers, taking fish, skinks, flying insects, or insects from the water surface. It also follows the plough on farms, feeding on exposed insects and earthworms. At sea, it eats mostly plankton. Its riverbed nesting sites are easily disturbed by people and off-road vehicles. When disturbed, the birds will dive-bomb intruders, but they can also end up abandoning their nests, so birdwatchers are asked to take special care. Farmers can help too by keeping sheep out of their nesting sites. Also known as inland tern or riverbed tern. The world population is about 5,000 birds.

Banded Rail / Moho Pererū

Rallus philippensis [Rallidae]

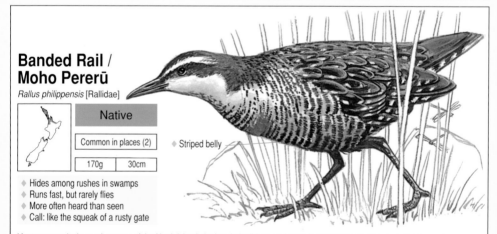

Native

Common in places (2)

♦ Striped belly

170g	30cm

♦ Hides among rushes in swamps
♦ Runs fast, but rarely flies
♦ More often heard than seen
♦ Call: like the squeak of a rusty gate

Most common in the northern part of the North Island, the banded rail lives and nests in saltmarsh, mangroves and some rush-covered freshwater swamps too. In tidal areas, it feeds mostly just after the high tide, making this a good time to look for them. Or just on dark. To get a glimpse of this secretive bird, try playing a recording of its call, or keep an eye out for its long-toed footprints in the mud. Its big feet help it to walk on this soft mud, where it goes looking for shellfish, crabs, spiders, insects and worms to eat, flicking its tail with each step. Although the banded rail can fly well, it is usually seen flying only short distances with its legs dangling. But proof of it once having been a good flier is the fact that other subspecies of the same bird are found naturally from Indonesia, the Philippines and Australia to as far east as Nuie. In Australia, the bird is much bolder and feeds unafraid along the roadside; in Vanuatu, it is caught and sold in the markets for food. The banded rail is closely related to the flightless weka (page 20) which is believed to be descended from the same ancestors. (In the South Island, a similar-looking bird, just one-quarter the size of the banded rail – the rare **marsh crake** – is sometimes seen.)

NZ Dabchick / Weweia

Poliocephalus rufopectus [Podicipedidae]

◆ Back rounded *(no tail)*

◆ Short, pointed bill

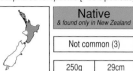

Native
& found only in New Zealand

Not common (3)	
250g	29cm

◆ **North Island only**
◆ Found mostly on shallow lakes
◆ Makes a little jump before it dives *(unlike scaup)*
◆ Half the weight of a scaup (page 59)

Most common on shallow lakes in central North Island, the dabchick is no longer found in the South Island. It often dives for 20-30 seconds at a time, eating mostly insects and freshwater snails, but also small fish, freshwater crayfish and tadpoles. Its floating nest is easily upset, so people using motorboats, water-skis and jet-skis are asked to take care on these lakes. While the newly hatched chicks (with their pretty zebra-striped head and neck) are able to swim and dive, they are also sometimes seen riding on their parents' back. Dabchicks have odd-looking lobed feet (not webbed like a duck) and cannot walk on land. When disturbed, they dive rather than flying like a duck and use another unusual defence of approaching backwards with its tail end fluffed up to show two white eye-like patterns. In winter dabchicks fly from one lake to another, but only at night. Dabchicks are in the same family as the Australasian Crested Grebe (page 61) and the much rarer **Australasian little grebe** (which is found only in Northland and north Canterbury).

◆ Pale wingtips (*unlike red-billed gull – page 75*)

◆ Long, thin, black bill (*orange with black tip, on young birds*)

Black-Billed Gull / Tarapunga

Larus bulleri [Laridae]

Native
& found only in New Zealand

Quite common (15)	
300/250g	37cm

◆ Compare with other gulls (pages 75 & 77)

Noticed in spring and summer along the braided shingle riverbeds of the eastern South Island, where tightly-packed colonies of up to 1,000 pairs of birds can be seen nesting. These nests can be vulnerable to floods, and predators. At the age of two or three days old, hungry chicks are already able to recognise the call of their own parents. Once the chick is able to swim, a few adult birds run crèches to protect the young birds, leaving other adults free to go out and feed. Hundreds of birds can sometimes be seen feeding together on worms, insects, fish and shellfish. In sand, they are seen rapidly paddling their feet up and down; this brings up marine worms which they like to eat. The black-billed gull is also found on lakes and nearby farmland, following the plough. In winter, it moves to the coast, often flying further north. They can live for over 18 years.

◆ Legs black (*pinkish on young birds*)

FRESHWATER

For easy comparison, the colour art on these two pages is all to the same scale: THIRD LIFE-SIZE

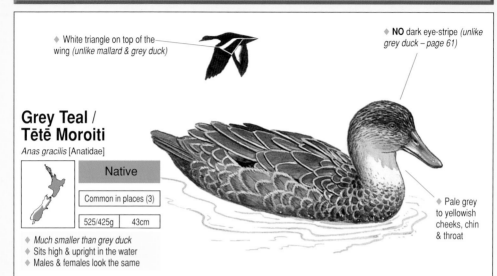

◆ White triangle on top of the wing *(unlike mallard & grey duck)*

◆ **NO** dark eye-stripe *(unlike grey duck – page 61)*

Grey Teal / Tētē Moroiti

Anas gracilis [Anatidae]

Native
Common in places (3)
525/425g	43cm

◆ *Much smaller than grey duck*
◆ Sits high & upright in the water
◆ Males & females look the same

◆ Pale grey to yellowish cheeks, chin & throat

Found on lakes and estuaries, the grey teal filters water insects (including mosquito larvae) from the water surface or from soft mud, and eats the seeds of water plants too. It rarely strays far from water. The grey teal is a protected bird but is often accidentally killed by duck shooters, mistaking it for the much larger grey duck. An Australian duck, the grey teal has become more common in New Zealand over the past fifty years, with the population increasing whenever Australian birds cross the Tasman Sea to escape severe droughts there. But, although some birds do clearly fly long distances, the grey teal doesn't generally travel far from home. They can form flocks of 10-50 birds, with groups of over 1,000 birds sometimes being seen in autumn. They can live to 21 years old. The slightly larger **brown teal** is very rare and confined mainly to Great Barrier Island.

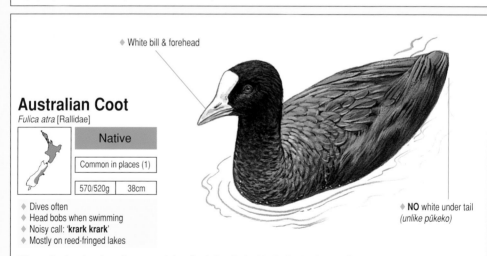

◆ White bill & forehead

Australian Coot

Fulica atra [Rallidae]

Native
Common in places (1)
570/520g	38cm

◆ Dives often
◆ Head bobs when swimming
◆ Noisy call: '**krark krark**'
◆ Mostly on reed-fringed lakes

◆ **NO** white under tail *(unlike pūkeko)*

This coot flew here from Australia, apparently breeding in New Zealand for the first time in 1958. Since then it has become common on many lakes and is still spreading. It builds a floating nest and can fly long distances between lakes at night, taking off from the water by pattering across the surface to get started, using its large feet with lobed toes. It will dive for up to 15 seconds to graze on underwater plants, although it does eat some insects too. Near some city lakes, it comes out of the water to eat grass. Other subspecies of the same bird are found in Europe, northern Africa, across Asia to Japan and New Guinea, so it is sometimes known as the Eurasian coot. It can live to over 18 years old. The larger, flightless, endemic **New Zealand coot** – once eaten by Māori – is thought to have been descended from an earlier invasion of the same bird; this is now extinct.

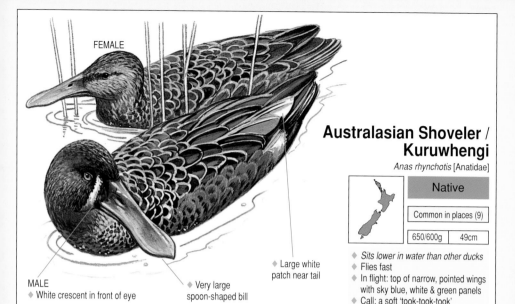

FEMALE

MALE
◆ White crescent in front of eye

◆ Very large spoon-shaped bill

◆ Large white patch near tail

Australasian Shoveler / Kuruwhengi

Anas rhynchotis [Anatidae]

Native
Common in places (9)

650/600g	49cm

◆ *Sits lower in water than other ducks*
◆ Flies fast
◆ In flight: top of narrow, pointed wings with sky blue, white & green panels
◆ Call: a soft 'took-took-took'

Found mostly in shallow, fertile wetlands or lakes with raupō (bulrushes). Unlike the grey duck and mallard, the shoveler is rarely seen away from water. This is because it cannot eat grass, for the comb-like sides of its bill and its bristle-fringed tongue are specially designed for sieving seeds, tiny water plants, freshwater insects and snails from the surface of the water. It is sometimes seen in flocks of several hundred birds. It regularly travels very long distances, many flying back and forth along the whole length of New Zealand. From March, the male displays its splendid breeding colours. The shoveler can be legally shot by licensed hunters during the duck-shooting season. It can live to over 11 years old. Australia and New Zealand each have their own subspecies. Australians know it as the blue-winged shoveler, because of the sky blue panels on the tops of its wings, visible when the bird is flying.

FEMALE
◆ Very dark brown

◆ White band on wings

MALE
◆ Glossy black with yellow eye

NZ Scaup / Pāpango

Aythya novaeseelandiae [Anatidae]

Native
& found only in New Zealand

Not common (5)

650g	40cm

◆ Shaped like a toy rubber duck
◆ NZ's only diving duck, diving without making a splash *(unlike dabchick)*
◆ Patters along the water to take off
◆ Flies fast, close to the water

Pronounced 'skawp', this bird uses its webbed feet to dive to depths of more than three metres to feed on water plants and freshwater snails on the bottom of deep, clean lakes. It can see well underwater, often diving for 15-20 seconds at a time (although able to stay down for over a minute). To resurface, it simply stops paddling, bobbing to the surface like a cork. The scaup can often be seen floating in large groups, with flocks of over 200 birds sometimes seen in autumn and winter. It is common on the Rotorua Lakes, Lake Taupo and many of the large, deep South Island lakes. To get a really good look at the bird, a telescope is useful. Also called black teal. The Māori name simply means black or dark coloured. It was hunted for food until protected in 1934.

FRESHWATER

For easy comparison, the colour art on these two pages is all to the same scale: QUARTER LIFE-SIZE

Blue Duck / Whio

Hymenolaimus malacorhynchos [Anatidae]

Native
& found only in New Zealand

Not common (3)

900/750g	53cm

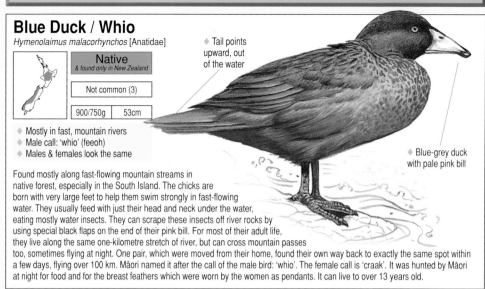

◆ Tail points
upward, out
of the water

◆ Blue-grey duck
with pale pink bill

◆ Mostly in fast, mountain rivers
◆ Male call: 'whio' (feeoh)
◆ Males & females look the same

Found mostly along fast-flowing mountain streams in
native forest, especially in the South Island. The chicks are
born with very large feet to help them swim strongly in fast-flowing
water. They usually feed with just their head and neck under the water,
eating mostly water insects. They can scrape these insects off river rocks by
using special black flaps on the end of their pink bill. For most of their adult life,
they live along the same one-kilometre stretch of river, but can cross mountain passes
too, sometimes flying at night. One pair, which were moved from their home, found their own way back to exactly the same spot within
a few days, flying over 100 km. Māori named it after the call of the male bird: 'whio'. The female call is 'craak'. It was hunted by Māori
at night for food and for the breast feathers which were worn by the women as pendants. It can live to over 13 years old.

Pūkeko

Porphyrio porphyrio [Rallidae]

Native

Common (35)

1050/850g	51cm

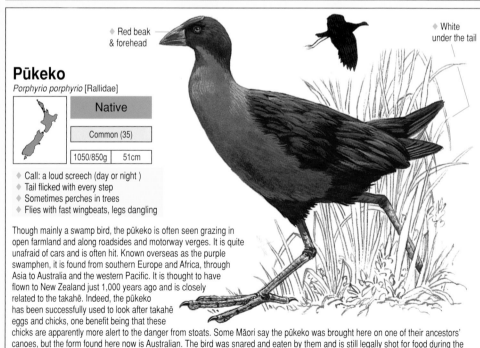

◆ Red beak
& forehead

◆ White
under the tail

◆ Call: a loud screech (day or night)
◆ Tail flicked with every step
◆ Sometimes perches in trees
◆ Flies with fast wingbeats, legs dangling

Though mainly a swamp bird, the pūkeko is often seen grazing in
open farmland and along roadsides and motorway verges. It is quite
unafraid of cars and is often hit. Known overseas as the purple
swamphen, it is found from southern Europe and Africa, through
Asia to Australia and the western Pacific. It is thought to have
flown to New Zealand just 1,000 years ago and is closely
related to the takahē. Indeed, the pūkeko
has been successfully used to look after takahē
eggs and chicks, one benefit being that these
chicks are apparently more alert to the danger from stoats. Some Māori say the pūkeko was brought here on one of their ancestors'
canoes, but the form found here now is Australian. The bird was snared and eaten by them and is still legally shot for food during the
duck-shooting season, although it is no longer a popular food. Māori used its feathers to decorate traditional flax cloaks. Pūkeko were
a pest in kūmara gardens, and remain a nuisance in some grain and vegetable growing areas today, where they frequently pull out
young plants. The pūkeko's diet consists of leaves, worms, insects, spiders, frogs and the chicks and eggs of ground-nesting birds.
They don't usually travel far, but one bird which was moved 96 km was able to find its own way home in eight days. Another banded
bird travelled 240 km. It can live to over 9 years old. The odd pūkeko can be part, or all, white (albino).

♦ Green panel on wings *(unlike mallard – next page)*

♦ Dark eye-stripe runs through eye *(unlike mallard & grey teal)*

Grey Duck / Pārera

Anas superciliosa [Anatidae]

Native
Common (30)

| 1100/1000g | 55cm |

♦ In pairs in remote areas; rare in parks & gardens *(unlike mallard)*
♦ Olive brown legs *(unlike mallard)*
♦ Males & females look the same

♦ Pale throat *(unlike mallard – next page)*

This used to be New Zealand's most common duck, but the introduced mallard (next page) has since taken over much of its habitat. These days, this native duck is mostly seen on small, shallow lakes and slow-flowing rivers in more remote areas. It can easily be confused with the female mallard and often interbreeds with it, producing birds which can be very hard to identify. It eats mainly seeds strained from the water through comb-like sieves at the sides of its bill, but also eats water plants, grass, water insects and small water snails. It can fly long distances, especially at night – occasionally to or from as far away as Australia. Hunted by early Māori and still legally shot by licensed hunters during the duck-shooting season. Since the 19th century it has been exported to Europe for lake bird collections. They can live to at least 20 years old. Found naturally also from Indonesia through Australia to the Pacific Islands. In Australia, it is known as the Pacific black duck.

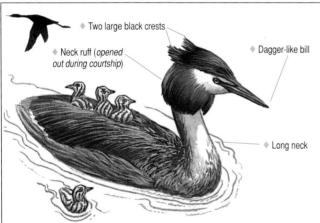

♦ Two large black crests

♦ Neck ruff *(opened out during courtship)*

♦ Dagger-like bill

Australasian Crested Grebe / Pūteketeke

Podiceps cristatus [Podicipedidae]

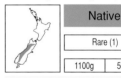

Native
Rare (1)

| 1100g | 50cm |

♦ **South Island only**
♦ Floats low in the water
♦ Dives without making a splash *(unlike diving ducks & shags)*
♦ Flies low over water with whirring wings, neck outstretched

♦ Long neck

This elegant bird is found on a few South Island lakes, such as Lake Alexandrina (near Lake Tekapo) and Lake Mapourika (West Coast). It cannot walk on land, so builds a floating nest which it anchors onto plants. People using motorboats, water-skis and jet-skis can help the grebe by taking care not to upset the birds and their nests along the shore with the wash from their craft. Grebe are often seen in pairs, feeding near rushes. They are good divers, staying underwater for 20 to 30 seconds – sometimes even 60 seconds – often resurfacing many metres from where they were last seen. In winter, they can swim beneath the ice for long distances using their odd-looking lobed feet, until they find small openings through which to re-emerge. They eat mainly fish and water insects, often swallowing their own feathers to mix with fish when feeding the chicks. These feathers help the chicks to cough up any sharp fish bones. The striped chicks can often be seen riding on their parents' backs. To impress a new mate, grebes perform a spectacular dance, nodding and shaking their heads to each other and doing a special 'penguin dance' by furiously paddling their feet. They were eaten by early Māori, but were given legal protection in 1885. Various subspecies of the same bird are found throughout Europe, Africa, and parts of Asia through to Australia. Overseas, they used to be killed for their breast feathers which were used to make 'grebe fur' muffs, capes and hats. (Each bird has around 20,000 feathers.) Also known as southern crested grebe or great crested grebe.

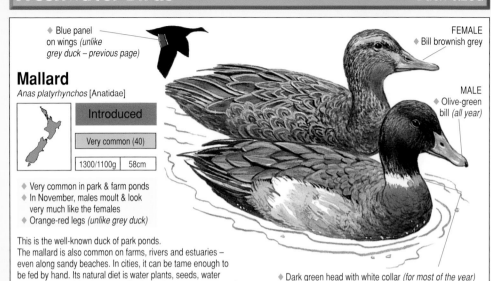

◆ Blue panel on wings *(unlike grey duck – previous page)*

FEMALE
◆ Bill brownish grey

Mallard
Anas platyrhynchos [Anatidae]

Introduced
Very common (40)

1300/1100g	58cm

◆ Very common in park & farm ponds
◆ In November, males moult & look very much like the females
◆ Orange-red legs *(unlike grey duck)*

MALE
◆ Olive-green bill *(all year)*

This is the well-known duck of park ponds. The mallard is also common on farms, rivers and estuaries – even along sandy beaches. In cities, it can be tame enough to be fed by hand. Its natural diet is water plants, seeds, water insects and small freshwater snails. But it also grazes grass and

◆ Dark green head with white collar *(for most of the year)*

clover and is sometimes a nuisance on farms, eating grains, peas and beans. The mallard is found naturally in Europe, Asia and North America, and was first brought here for sport from Britain in the 1860s and later again from the USA. It can sometimes interbreed with the native grey duck (page 61), producing birds which can be hard to identify. In December and January, when mallards are moulting, they can be seen in large flightless flocks of up to 1,000 birds or more. They can live to over 26 years old.

MALE
◆ Black *(all year)*

Paradise Shelduck / Pūtangitangi
Tadorna variegata [Anatidae]

Native
& found only in New Zealand

Common (35)

1700/1400g	63cm

◆ Large, goose-like duck
◆ Usually seen in pairs
◆ Male call: **'klonk'**; female call: **'zeek'**
◆ In flight: large white patch on wing
◆ Young females have white eye-patch

FEMALE
◆ White head & neck *(all year)*

'Parries' are often seen on farmland, especially in hill country, but also on lakes, ponds, coastal flats and high-country riverbeds. Large flocks of 1,000 birds or more are sometimes seen from December to March, when they are moulting and unable to fly. (A young friend refers to such paradise ducks as 'paralysed ducks'!) They eat grass and clover, water plants and seeds. Paradise shelducks usually nest in a dip or hole in the ground or in a hollow log. But some birds nest in trees up 25 metres off the ground, leaving the ducklings to make a long leap to the ground. When the ducklings hatch, they are covered in brown and white zebra-stripes. Once able to fly, they may travel over 200 km from their birthplace, but as adults they tend to stay in the same area. Paradise shelducks were an important food of early Māori and were later hunted for sale at the Wellington market. Māori women wore the mottled feathers as pendants or necklaces. Live birds were also exported for waterfowl collections in park lakes overseas. They can live to at least 23 years old. ('Shelduck' is the name given to a particular group of large goose-like ducks.)

White-Faced Heron / Matuku Moana
Go to page 80

Little Shag / Kawau Paka
(About duck-sized. Can be black & white or all black. Short yellow bill.)
Go to page 78

Little Black Shag / Kawau Tuī
(About duck-sized. Always glossy black with grey bill.)
Go to page 78

FRESHWATER

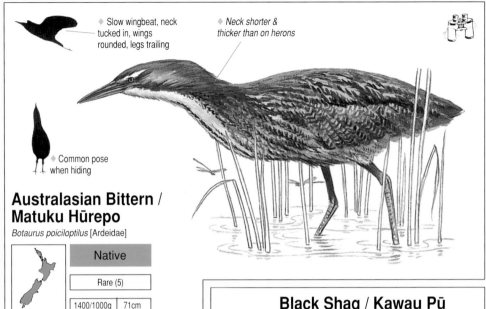

◆ Slow wingbeat, neck tucked in, wings rounded, legs trailing

◆ Neck shorter & thicker than on herons

◆ Common pose when hiding

Australasian Bittern / Matuku Hūrepo

Botaurus poiciloptilus [Ardeidae]

Native		
Rare (5)		
1400/1000g	71cm	

◆ More often heard than seen
◆ Male call: loud booming, like a foghorn (evenings & early mornings June-Feb)
◆ Often hunched when feeding

The bittern usually stays well-hidden among tall, dense, wetland reeds, but sometimes comes out into damp hollows in open pasture. If disturbed, it stands frozen with its bill pointing to the sky, its streaked feathers making it look like a stick or a clump of reeds. Like this, it will sometimes even sway with the wind. Its eyes are strangely arranged so that it can still see in all directions from this position. In the evenings and early mornings, from mid-winter to late summer, the male marks its territory by making deep booming calls every 15 or 30 minutes – a weird call which sounds like a distant foghorn, like someone blowing across the mouth of a bottle, or like the bellow of a bull. The bittern is usually seen at dawn and dusk as it feeds mostly at night, eating eels, frogs, mice, rats, freshwater crayfish and water insects. But it is sometimes seen in the middle of the day too. It was far more common before most wetlands were drained for farming. Farmers can help to protect its remaining habitat by fencing grazing cattle out of these wetlands. Early Māori valued its feathers, presenting these in ornate boxes as gifts. As recently as the mid 1900s, the bittern was being killed by fishermen who used its feathers as trout flies. As its common name suggests, this bird is found in Australia too. Matuku is a general Māori name for herons. The endemic **New Zealand little bittern** (**kaoriki**) became extinct in the late 1800s.

Black Shag / Kawau Pū

(Larger than a duck. Front always black.)

Go to page 79

♦ White chin strap

♦ *Shorter neck than a swan*

Canada Goose
Branta canadensis [Anatidae]

Introduced
Common in places (5)

5400/4500g	83cm

♦ Flies with neck outstretched
♦ Flocks fly in V formation
♦ Call: a loud double honk

Nicknamed 'honker' after its loud call. Much more common in the South Island, particularly in high-country farmland, lakes and rivers. In summer, many move to coastal lakes and estuaries for the autumn moulting season, gathering in noisy flocks of up to 2,000 or more birds. It eats grass, clover and water plants. Since sheep and cattle can be reluctant to graze where geese have been feeding, many thousands of geese are sometimes shot, especially when the birds are moulting and unable to fly. Like swans, the Canada goose looks after its chicks in crèches – with up to fifty birds per crèche. Naturally found in North America and north eastern Asia and brought to New Zealand from North America between 1905 and 1920 for hunters to shoot at. They can live to over 30 years old. New Zealand had two endemic **giant flightless geese** of its own, about twice the size of the Canada goose. These are thought to have become extinct during Māori settlement, possibly as a result of being hunted for food.

FRESHWATER

◆ Flies with long neck outstretched, slow wingbeats, showing white wing feathers

◆ Very long neck

◆ Red bill with white patch

Black Swan

Cygnus atratus [Anatidae]

Introduced	
Quite common (15)	
6000/5000g	120cm

◆ Call: a loud musical bugling (day or night)

A majestic bird, usually seen on lakes, estuaries and in city parks, but also sometimes at sea or on farmland. Occasionally seen in spectacular flocks of several thousand birds. Black swans are vegetarians, eating mainly underwater plants. In lakes, their long necks allow them to reach plants deeper into the lake than ducks, so swans often end up out-competing other water birds and driving them away. After heavy rains, lake water levels can be so high that the up-ended swan can no longer reach the bottom and will come out onto farmland to graze on clover and grass, making them a nuisance to farmers. On Rotorua lakes, the birds sometimes find the webbing between their toes dissolving in the acid or alkaline thermal waters. It can be five months before the chicks can fly, so adults run crèches, looking after up to forty chicks at a time. The black swan was introduced from Australia to New Zealand in the 1860s for hunting, though some birds may have flown over by themselves and may even still make this long trans-Tasman flight. Can live to 29 years. The rarer **mute swan** (a white swan with an orange bill) is found in Hawke's Bay and near Christchurch. An endemic **New Zealand swan** was hunted for food by early Māori but is now extinct; it was very similar to the black swan of today.

Seashore Birds

(Birds of beaches, rocky shore & estuaries)

New Zealand is a seabird nation; its seas are among the richest in the world, both for variety of species and for sheer number of birds. Most are native and many are not found anywhere else in the world (endemic).

Ocean Birds. About one third of New Zealand's birds (more than 100 species) are true ocean-going birds. Many look so similar that even the experts have trouble telling them apart. So skuas, petrels, prions and shearwaters are not included. (See Further Reading, page 93.)

Waders. Over 50 species of wading birds have been seen in New Zealand, many of them rare summer visitors. Only common waders are covered.

Some of the birds seen along the shore are more common inland so are covered in more detail elsewhere in the book, but all birds seen here are shown together in the picture keys on the following pages.

TIPS for Birdwatching at the Seashore

◆ On sand spits and beaches, take care not to disturb nesting birds or step on their eggs. It is better to watch from a distance, especially from the other side of a stream or channel, where you will not make the birds nervous.

◆ Estuaries and cliff tops are usually better spots than beaches for birdwatching. (See sites marked in yellow on the birdwatching hot spots map, page 92.)

◆ On estuaries, the birds spread out to feed when the tide is out. When the tide returns, they gather at a safe place to rest. This means that high tide is usually an easier time to get a good look at them.

◆ Binoculars (or a telescope) are particularly handy on the shore.

◆ At night, nesting colonies of seabirds can sometimes be heard, eg **grey-faced petrels** in the North Island or **sooty shearwaters** on Stewart Island.

KEY: Seashore Birds often Found by their Call (Common night calls)

	page	
Pied Stilt	74	Barking or yapping call *(sometimes while flying overhead)*
Oystercatchers	76	A loud, shrill: 'kleep'
Spur-Winged Plover	46	Loud '**kitter kitter kitter**' *(sometimes while flying overhead)*
Penguins	82	Mewing, trumpeting, screaming or growling *(when nesting)*

KEY: BIRDS of SANDY BEACHES

The birds are placed in this picture according to where they are most likely to be seen.
Shrubby dunes can often be a good bird habitat too, with finches, magpie, quail and pheasant.
The birds are arranged in order of size, with the smallest bird in each group at the top left.

Flying & diving off-shore

Wht-Front Tern	Caspian Tern	Gannet
page 74	page 76	page 83

On the beach

Chaffinch	Sparrow	Pipit	Band Dotterel	Blk-Front Tern	Starling
page 38	page 40	page 41	page 72	page 56	page 42

(North Island only)

Myna	NZ Dotterel	Wht-Front Tern	Black-Bill Gull	Red-Bill Gull	Spur-Wing Plover
page 44	page 73	page 74	page 57	page 75	page 46

(not in spring)

P Oystercatcher	Caspian Tern	V Oystercatcher	Black-Back Gull	Pied Shag	Black Shag
page 76	page 76	page 77	page 77	page 79	page 79

Flying over sand dunes

Swallow	Skylark	Harrier
page 54	page 41	page 48

68

KEY: BIRDS of ROCKY SHORE

The birds are placed in this picture according to where they are most likely to be seen.
They are arranged in order of size, with the smallest bird in each group at the left.

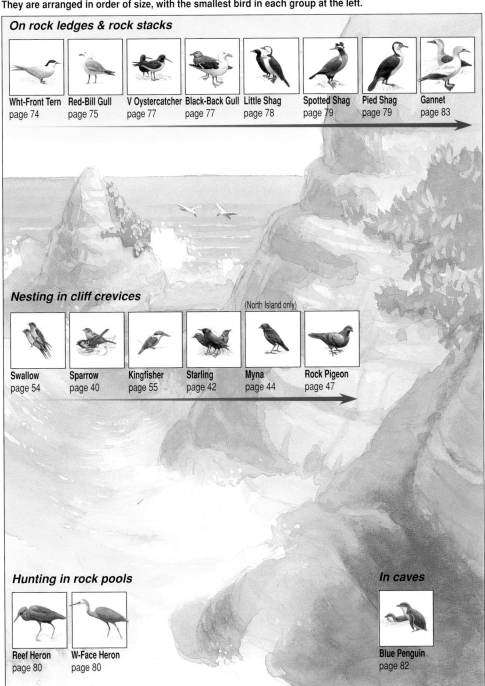

On rock ledges & rock stacks

Wht-Front Tern	Red-Bill Gull	V Oystercatcher	Black-Back Gull	Little Shag	Spotted Shag	Pied Shag	Gannet
page 74	page 75	page 77	page 77	page 78	page 79	page 79	page 83

Nesting in cliff crevices

(North Island only)

Swallow	Sparrow	Kingfisher	Starling	Myna	Rock Pigeon
page 54	page 40	page 55	page 42	page 44	page 47

Hunting in rock pools

Reef Heron	W-Face Heron
page 80	page 80

In caves

Blue Penguin
page 82

KEY: BIRDS of ESTUARIES

The birds are placed in this picture according to where they are most likely to be seen.
They are arranged in order of size, with the smallest bird in each group at the left.

Flying overhead (in search of food)

Swallow page 54	**Wht-Front Tern** page 74	**Caspian Tern** page 76	**Harrier** page 48

Afloat

Grey Teal page 58	**Shoveler** page 59	**Grey Duck** page 61	**Mallard** page 62	**Canada Goose** page 65	**Black Swan** page 66

Wading Birds
(autumn & winter)

Wrybill page 72	**Band Dotterel** page 72	**Knot** page 73	**NZ Dotterel** page 73	**Pied Stilt** page 74	**Godwit** page 75	**S-W Plover** page 46	**Reef Heron** page 80

Standing near the water's edge
(autumn & winter)　　　　(winter)

Blk-Front Tern page 56	**Wht-Front Tern** page 74	**Black-Bill Gull** page 57	**Red-Bill Gull** page 75	**Caspian Tern** page 76	**Black-Back Gull** page 77

70

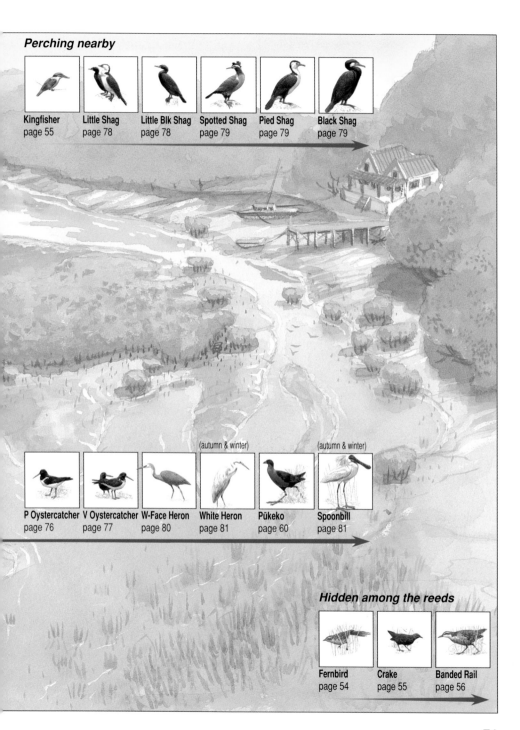

Perching nearby

Kingfisher
page 55

Little Shag
page 78

Little Blk Shag
page 78

Spotted Shag
page 79

Pied Shag
page 79

Black Shag
page 79

P Oystercatcher
page 76

V Oystercatcher
page 77

W-Face Heron
page 80

(autumn & winter)
White Heron
page 81

Pūkeko
page 60

(autumn & winter)
Spoonbill
page 81

Hidden among the reeds

Fernbird
page 54

Crake
page 55

Banded Rail
page 56

Pale grey back *(most useful tip for identifying them on estuaries)*

Bill curves to the right *(but hard to see without a telescope)*

BREEDING ADULT
Black collar *(most useful tip for identifying them on riverbeds)*

Wrybill / Ngutu Parore
Anarhynchus frontalis [Charadriidae]

Native
& found only in New Zealand

Common in places (3)

60g	20cm

- On mudflats, it runs & pauses, sweeping its bill sideways to feed
- Often stands on one leg

Unique in the world, the wrybill is the only bird with a bill which curves sideways – very useful when stooping to feed on insects hidden beneath river stones. In spring, it nests on the wide, shingle riverbeds of eastern South Island, but around Christmas it migrates to North Island estuaries, where it feeds on wet mudflats, especially in the Firth of Thames (Miranda) and on the Manukau and Kaipara Harbours. Here, it meets up with Arctic waders which have travelled twenty times as far from the Arctic north. In these mudflats, the wrybill feeds on sandhoppers and mudworms etc. At high tide, the birds form dense flocks on the ground, usually away from other birds, often with every wrybill standing on one leg. In mid-August, when they are about to leave again for the South Island, the birds peel off the ground as one flock like a scarf unfurling in the wind. They then return to the upper Waitaki, Rakaia, Ahuriri and Cass Rivers to breed. Here, male birds make a nest by simply bulldozing a hollow in the shingle with their breast; in it, a female lays two grey shingle-coloured eggs. In the North Island, they are easily seen near the Miranda Shorebird Centre, south of Auckland. They can live to 17 years old. Found only in New Zealand, with a population of about 5,000 birds.

Banded Dotterel / Pohowera
Charadrius bicinctus [Charadriidae]

Native
& breeds only in New Zealand

Quite common (15)

60g	20cm

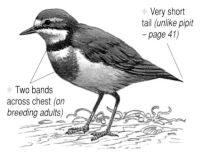

Very short tail *(unlike pipit – page 41)*

Two bands across chest *(on breeding adults)*

- *Much smaller than NZ dotterel (opposite)*
- Runs, stops, then bobs up & down
- Call: 'pit pit' (high pitched)

Banded dotterel are seen along sandy beaches and shell-banks, sometimes also on farmland and airfields. Most breed on the wide, shingle riverbeds of the South Island and southern North Island, migrating to northern New Zealand in February. A few nest on northern beaches and in the Rangipo Desert in central North Island. Others prefer South Island high country and many of these high country birds are known to migrate in March to south eastern Australia, just as the gannet and white-fronted tern do. Banded dotterel nest in a simple dip in the sand or shingle. They eat insects, earthworms and some berries. On dry sand flats, they find their food by running, stopping, looking, stepping, then pecking. On wet sand, they simply run, stop and peck. They can also sometimes be seen trembling one foot on the ground to encourage creatures to the surface. Large winter flocks can be seen by the Miranda Shorebird Centre, near Auckland. The birds can live to over 10 years old. A smaller Australian relative, the **black-fronted dotterel** is also sometimes seen on shingle riverbeds.

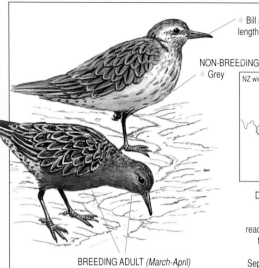

Bill about same length as head

NON-BREEDING
Grey

NZ winter

NZ summer

Lesser Knot / Huahou
Calidris canutus [Scolopacidae]

Regular Visitor

Common in places (2)

| 120g | 24cm |

- Usually seen in flocks, often along with godwits (page 75)
- Most common in NZ Sep – March

BREEDING ADULT *(March-April)*
Rusty red head & chest

During the long days of the Arctic summer, the lesser knot breeds near the coasts of the Arctic Ocean. But, before the Arctic winter sets in, it flies south, many birds from eastern Siberia eventually reaching here to feed during the New Zealand summer. To complete this incredible journey of about 16,000 km, most lesser knots are believed to stop just twice along the way to feed, arriving here in September and October. In March and April, the birds head back on their long flight north, returning to the melting snows of Siberia via northern Australia and a month-long refuelling stop on the coast of China or Korea. In New Zealand, knots are often seen resting in large tight flocks, along with the much-larger godwits. When taking off, they seem to peel off the ground like a scarf in the wind. The name 'knot' comes from 'Canute' for, like King Canute, knots stand in the rising tide, as if refusing to budge. As the tide falls, they spread out to begin feeding again, drilling the soft mud or wet sand like a sewing machine, eating mostly small shellfish. Though found on estuaries throughout New Zealand, they are more common in the north. Easily seen near the Miranda Shorebird Centre, south of Auckland, but also common on the Kaipara Harbour, Manukau Harbour and Farewell Spit. Some birds stay behind in New Zealand through our winter. It is also known simply as knot, or red knot – from its breeding colours.

Large eye

Larger bill than banded dotterel *(opposite)*

Rusty orange below *(non-breeding birds are white below)*

NZ Dotterel / Tūturiwhatu
Charadrius obscurus [Charadriidae]

Native
& found only in New Zealand

Not common (4)

| 160g | 25cm |

- About the size of a plump blackbird
- Walks or runs, then stops & pecks to feed
- Often come up close on the beach
- Often heard making a loud: 'chip'

In spring, the New Zealand dotterel makes its nest on a sandy beach, in a shallow dip in the sand just above high tide, often near the mouth of a stream, next to a small landmark like a plant or piece of wood. As numbers have been dropping, some breeding sites are fenced off each summer and signposted to protect them from dogs and holiday makers. The New Zealand dotterel is also threatened by hedgehogs eating its eggs, so stoats and wild cats, so these animals all need to be controlled too. While some birds stay on these beaches all year, others move off in late summer to a nearby estuary, where they can be seen in small flocks. They live on insects, sandhoppers, crabs, shellfish and small fish. A good spot to see the birds is near the Miranda Shorebird Centre, south of Auckland, but also at many Northland, Coromandel, or Bay of Plenty beaches. It is found only in New Zealand and is believed to be descended from an earlier invasion of the same ancestors as the banded dotterel (opposite). They can live to over 30 years old. A rarer subspecies is found on the beaches and mountain tops of Stewart Island.

SEASHORE

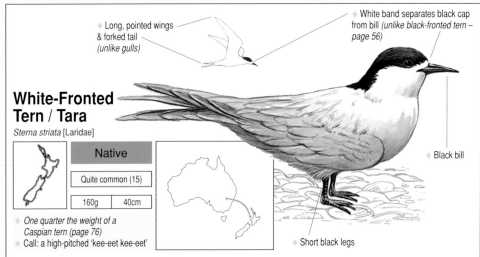

◆ Long, pointed wings & forked tail (unlike gulls)

◆ White band separates black cap from bill (unlike black-fronted tern – page 56)

White-Fronted Tern / Tara

Sterna striata [Laridae]

Native	
Quite common (15)	
160g	40cm

◆ One quarter the weight of a Caspian tern (page 76)
◆ Call: a high-pitched 'kee-eet kee-eet'

◆ Black bill

◆ Short black legs

New Zealand's most common seashore tern, the white-fronted tern swirls along with gulls just off the coast in large flocks. Flying close to the water surface, it picks out small fish from shoals driven to the surface by hungry kahawai, so is sometimes known as the 'kahawai bird'. On its own, it will hover, then dive. Just as it tries to swallow its catch, it is then often chased by thieving gulls and **skuas**. Large, tightly-packed colonies of up to 2,000 birds can be seen facing into the wind on sand spits and beaches (often along with red-billed gulls). Some nest on rock stacks, steep cliffs and islands. Its eggs were eaten by early Māori. In autumn, many adult white-fronted terns and most young birds migrate across the Tasman Sea to spend their winter in south eastern Australia. Sometimes also known as sea swallow. They can live to over 26 years old.

Pied Stilt / Poaka

Himantopus himantopus [Recurvirostridae]

Native	
Common (35)	
190g	35cm

◆ Often calls while flying *(day or night)*
◆ Call: a high-pitched yap or bark

◆ Long legs trail behind

◆ Very long black bill

◆ Very long pink legs

The pied stilt is thought to have flown to New Zealand from Australia, establishing itself here since Europeans arrived – as recently as the early 1800s. In shallow water or on wet ground, it appears to be standing on stilts as it feeds in noisy flocks, eating insects, worms and shellfish. Along the coast, it feeds mostly at low tide, regardless of whether it is day or night. The stilt nests in open areas, in loose colonies on gravel riverbeds and near wetlands, often making a simple scrape in the ground, but also sometimes building itself a large platform nest. If you get too close to a nest, a parent bird will often try to lure you away by pretending to be wounded. During summer nights, riverbed birds are often heard 'barking' as they fly overhead, migrating down to the coast. The same bird is found throughout the warmer countries of the world, where it is known as the black-winged stilt. It can live to about 12 years old. In parts of the eastern South Island, it can interbreed with the endangered **black stilt** (the rarest wader in the world). The interbred offspring are pied stilts with darker colourings and such 'crosses' are not uncommon.

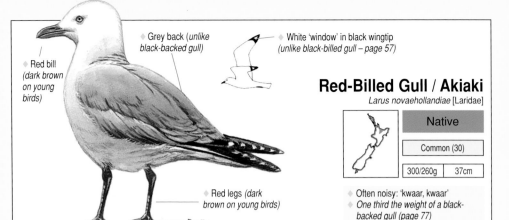

◆ Grey back (*unlike black-backed gull*)

◆ White 'window' in black wingtip (*unlike black-billed gull – page 57*)

◆ Red bill (*dark brown on young birds*)

Red-Billed Gull / Akiaki
Larus novaehollandiae [Laridae]

Native	
Common (30)	
300/260g	37cm

◆ Red legs (*dark brown on young birds*)

◆ Often noisy: 'kwaar, kwaar'
◆ One third the weight of a black-backed gull (page 77)

The common red-billed gull is often seen in large flocks on, or near, the coast. It is occasionally seen inland too – especially near Rotorua, where birds can find the webbing between their toes dissolved in the acid or alkaline thermal waters. This gull will follow ships into deep water, but rarely leaves sight of land. Its diet includes a wide range of seafood, as well as worms, insects and even berries. It often steals food from other birds and can sometimes be seen paddling its feet up and down in sand to bring up marine worms to eat.

The red-billed gull is a useful beach cleaner and one bird which has benefited from the arrival of people in New Zealand, for it often feeds on scraps from fishing boats, meatworks, rubbish tips and around supermarkets too. It is a common bird in parks and streets of coastal cities. Tight colonies of up to 6,000 pairs of birds will sometimes nest on sand spits and beaches, but this gull usually nests in much smaller colonies on headlands and remote off-shore islands – which are, of course, much safer places for them. They can live to at least 28 years old. Other subspecies of the same bird are found in South Africa, Australia and the south-western Pacific.

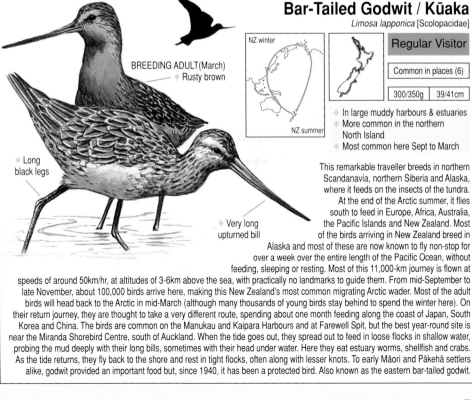

Bar-Tailed Godwit / Kūaka
Limosa lapponica [Scolopacidae]

NZ winter

NZ summer

BREEDING ADULT (March)
◆ Rusty brown

Regular Visitor	
Common in places (6)	
300/350g	39/41cm

◆ In large muddy harbours & estuaries
◆ More common in the northern North Island
◆ Most common here Sept to March

◆ Long black legs

◆ Very long upturned bill

This remarkable traveller breeds in northern Scandanavia, northern Siberia and Alaska, where it feeds on the insects of the tundra. At the end of the Arctic summer, it flies south to feed in Europe, Africa, Australia, the Pacific Islands and New Zealand. Most of the birds arriving in New Zealand breed in Alaska and most of these are now known to fly non-stop for over a week over the entire length of the Pacific Ocean, without feeding, sleeping or resting. Most of this 11,000-km journey is flown at speeds of around 50km/hr, at altitudes of 3-6km above the sea, with practically no landmarks to guide them. From mid-September to late November, about 100,000 birds arrive here, making this New Zealand's most common migrating Arctic wader. Most of the adult birds will head back to the Arctic in mid-March (although many thousands of young birds stay behind to spend the winter here). On their return journey, they are thought to take a very different route, spending about one month feeding along the coast of Japan, South Korea and China. The birds are common on the Manukau and Kaipara Harbours and at Farewell Spit, but the best year-round site is near the Miranda Shorebird Centre, south of Auckland. When the tide goes out, they spread out to feed in loose flocks in shallow water, probing the mud deeply with their long bills, sometimes with their head under water. Here they eat estuary worms, shellfish and crabs. As the tide returns, they fly back to the shore and rest in tight flocks, often along with lesser knots. To early Māori and Pākehā settlers alike, godwit provided an important food but, since 1940, it has been a protected bird. Also known as the eastern bar-tailed godwit.

SEASHORE

For easy comparison, the colour art on these two pages is all to the same scale: QUARTER LIFE-SIZE

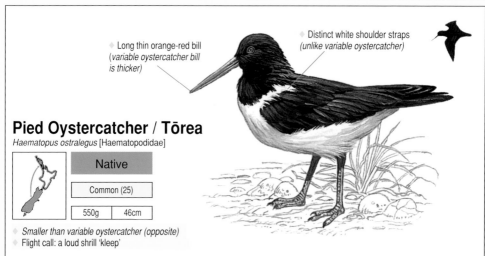

Long thin orange-red bill
(*variable oystercatcher bill
is thicker*)

Distinct white shoulder straps
(*unlike variable oystercatcher*)

Pied Oystercatcher / Tōrea

Haematopus ostralegus [Haematopodidae]

Native	
Common (25)	
550g	46cm

◆ *Smaller than variable oystercatcher (opposite)*
◆ Flight call: a loud shrill 'kleep'

Common on estuaries, sandy beaches, farmland and riverbeds, picking food from the surface or pushing its bill deep underground. It eats shellfish, worms, insects and small fish, opening shellfish either by hammering it or levering the shells open with its strong bill. From late summer to the end of winter, it is common on the Kaipara and Manukau Harbours and can easily be seen near the Miranda Shorebird Centre, south of Auckland. From August, most head south to nest on the braided riverbeds and farms of the eastern South Island. It is then very common along roadsides near Invercargill and sometimes has to be chased off sports fields before the games can begin. In January, most birds migrate back to estuaries and sandy beaches around the North Island. To Māori, oystercatchers warned of coming storms. From about 1885, these birds were hunted for food by Europeans and all but disappeared until the shooting of shorebirds was banned in 1940. They can live to over 27 years old. Also called SIPO from its old name of South Island pied oystercatcher. Found along coasts throughout most of the world, although New Zealand has its own subspecies.

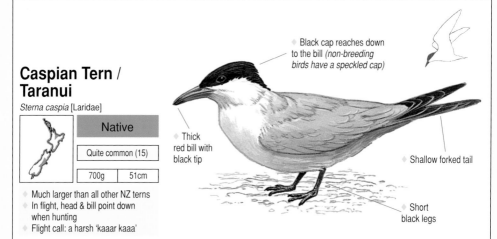

Black cap reaches down
to the bill (*non-breeding
birds have a speckled cap*)

Caspian Tern / Taranui

Sterna caspia [Laridae]

Native	
Quite common (15)	
700g	51cm

Thick
red bill with
black tip

Shallow forked tail

◆ Much larger than all other NZ terns
◆ In flight, head & bill point down
   when hunting
◆ Flight call: a harsh 'kaaar kaaa'

Short
black legs

Though a native of New Zealand and found throughout most of the world, the first birds to be studied were from the Caspian Sea, hence the common name. The Caspian tern is more common in the north of New Zealand. In coastal waters, single birds are often seen flying with their heads down, looking out for small fish. It hovers, then drops into a sudden dive, often disappearing underwater like a gannet. A few birds travel up rivers or feed over lakes. In spring, they nest on quiet sand spits and shell-banks in large loose colonies of up to 100 pairs or more. Some of these colonies are fenced to protect the birds from off-road vehicles, people and dogs. The Caspian tern is thought to have arrived in New Zealand about 1860 – since European settlement. It can live to over 24 years old.

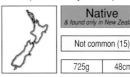

BLACK & WHITE BIRDS have
smudgy border between the colours
(unlike pied oystercatcher – opposite)

Variable Oystercatcher /
Tōrea Pango

Haematopus unicolor [Haematopodidae]

Native	
& found only in New Zealand	
Not common (15)	
725g	48cm

Long orange-
red bill *(thicker
than on pied
oystercatcher)*

◆ Some birds
are ALL BLACK

◆ *Larger than pied oystercatcher
(opposite)*
◆ Flight call: a loud shrill 'kleep'

Unlike the pied oystercatcher, the variable oystercatcher is found only along the coast, mostly on sandy beaches and estuaries, but also along rocky coasts, usually in pairs but sometimes in small flocks. Only half the birds in the northern North Island are pure black, but in the southern South Island almost all are black. This is thought to be because birds in the cooler south need to absorb more of the sun's heat to keep warm, for black is better for absorbing radiated heat. They eat shellfish, worms, crabs and small fish, and used to be hunted by Europeans for food until they were protected in 1940. Its nest is simply a scrape in the sand just above high tide, often on a sand spit. Here, pairs often nest in the same weeks in which most New Zealanders take their annual holidays (around Christmas), so need special protection from predators and people. They can live to over 19 years old. The world population is about 4,000 birds.

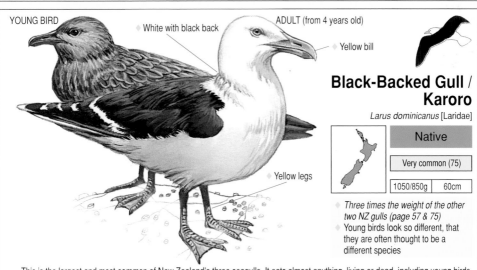

YOUNG BIRD

White with black back

ADULT (from 4 years old)

Yellow bill

Black-Backed Gull /
Karoro

Larus dominicanus [Laridae]

Native	
Very common (75)	
1050/850g	60cm

Yellow legs

◆ *Three times the weight of the other
two NZ gulls (page 57 & 75)*
◆ Young birds look so different, that
they are often thought to be a
different species

This is the largest and most common of New Zealand's three seagulls. It eats almost anything, living or dead, including young birds, even new-born lambs or sick sheep. It is not only seen on beaches and harbours, but also following boats, in city parks, farmland, riverbeds, near lakes, even high in the mountains, far above the tree line. It is common too around meatworks, sewer outfalls, rubbish dumps and supermarkets and is often spotted perching on street lamps. It has been known to eat its own eggs and chicks, and has been seen taking on birds as large as harriers – on at least one occasion holding one under water and drowning it. It is one of the few native New Zealand birds which is not protected by law. Māori tamed these gulls for use in natural pest control, for the gulls eat the large caterpillars which damaged kūmara crops, and tame birds are still sometimes used to rid city gardens of snails. It usually nests in colonies, on sand spits or beaches, along inland riverbeds and lake shores, but sometimes also on the roofs of city buildings. The mottled brown young bird is known to Māori as ngōiro, and it is not hard to see why many people think it is a different bird. It is not until it is four years old (when it turns black and white) that it breeds. Black-backed gulls can live to 28 years old. It is also sometimes called the Dominican gull from the colours worn by Dominican friars. Many people also call it 'mollyhawk', an apparent confusion between harrier hawk and mollymawk (a small albatross). The same gull is found from South Africa and South America to the Antarctic coast.

SEASHORE

For easy comparison, the colour art on these two pages is all to the same scale: SIXTH LIFE-SIZE

Seashore Birds: Shags

◆ SWIM with body low in the water & head tilted up DIVING for fish
◆ IN FLIGHT: Fast wingbeats, neck outstretched
◆ OFTEN PERCH on posts with wings stretched out to dry

About the size of a common duck
◆ If any white = **Little Shag**
◆ If all black, then look at the bill >>>
◆ A short yellow bill = **Little Shag**
◆ A long, thin, dark grey bill = **Little Black Shag**

Larger than a common duck
◆ A black front = **Black Shag**
◆ A white front = **Pied Shag**
◆ Grey with yellow feet = **Spotted Shag**

Shags use their webbed feet to swim and dive, and nest on an untidy platform of sticks or seaweed. Also known as cormorants. 12 species breed in New Zealand, but many of these are found only on outlying islands, one on and around Stewart Island.

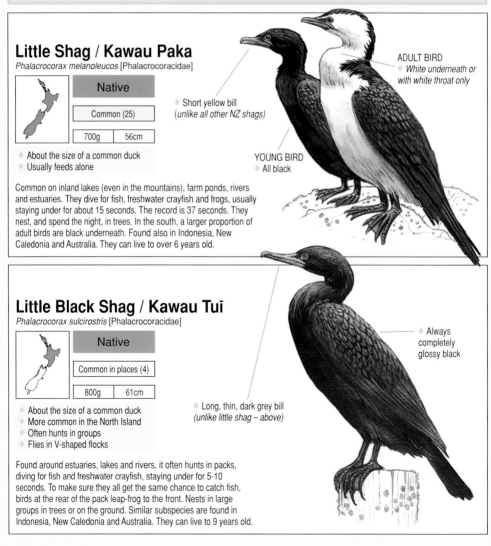

Little Shag / Kawau Paka
Phalacrocorax melanoleucos [Phalacrocoracidae]

Native	
Common (25)	
700g	56cm

◆ About the size of a common duck
◆ Usually feeds alone

◆ Short yellow bill
(unlike all other NZ shags)

ADULT BIRD
◆ *White underneath or with white throat only*

YOUNG BIRD
◆ All black

Common on inland lakes (even in the mountains), farm ponds, rivers and estuaries. They dive for fish, freshwater crayfish and frogs, usually staying under for about 15 seconds. The record is 37 seconds. They nest, and spend the night, in trees. In the south, a larger proportion of adult birds are black underneath. Found also in Indonesia, New Caledonia and Australia. They can live to over 6 years old.

Little Black Shag / Kawau Tuī
Phalacrocorax sulcirostris [Phalacrocoracidae]

Native	
Common in places (4)	
800g	61cm

◆ About the size of a common duck
◆ More common in the North Island
◆ Often hunts in groups
◆ Flies in V-shaped flocks

◆ Always completely glossy black

◆ Long, thin, dark grey bill
(unlike little shag – above)

Found around estuaries, lakes and rivers, it often hunts in packs, diving for fish and freshwater crayfish, staying under for 5-10 seconds. To make sure they all get the same chance to catch fish, birds at the rear of the pack leap-frog to the front. Nests in large groups in trees or on the ground. Similar subspecies are found in Indonesia, New Caledonia and Australia. They can live to 9 years old.

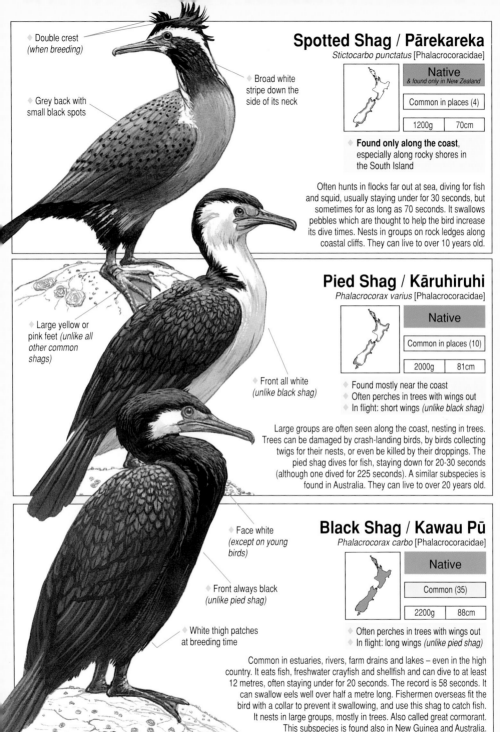

Spotted Shag / Pārekareka
Stictocarbo punctatus [Phalacrocoracidae]

Native	
& found only in New Zealand	
Common in places (4)	
1200g	70cm

◆ Double crest
(when breeding)

◆ Broad white
stripe down the
side of its neck

◆ Grey back with
small black spots

◆ **Found only along the coast**,
especially along rocky shores in
the South Island

Often hunts in flocks far out at sea, diving for fish
and squid, usually staying under for 30 seconds, but
sometimes for as long as 70 seconds. It swallows
pebbles which are thought to help the bird increase
its dive times. Nests in groups on rock ledges along
coastal cliffs. They can live to over 10 years old.

Pied Shag / Kāruhiruhi
Phalacrocorax varius [Phalacrocoracidae]

Native	
Common in places (10)	
2000g	81cm

◆ Large yellow or
pink feet *(unlike all
other common
shags)*

◆ Front all white
(unlike black shag)

◆ Found mostly near the coast
◆ Often perches in trees with wings out
◆ In flight: short wings *(unlike black shag)*

Large groups are often seen along the coast, nesting in trees.
Trees can be damaged by crash-landing birds, by birds collecting
twigs for their nests, or even be killed by their droppings. The
pied shag dives for fish, staying down for 20-30 seconds
(although one dived for 225 seconds). A similar subspecies is
found in Australia. They can live to over 20 years old.

Black Shag / Kawau Pū
Phalacrocorax carbo [Phalacrocoracidae]

Native	
Common (35)	
2200g	88cm

◆ Face white
*(except on young
birds)*

◆ Front always black
(unlike pied shag)

◆ White thigh patches
at breeding time

◆ Often perches in trees with wings out
◆ In flight: long wings *(unlike pied shag)*

Common in estuaries, rivers, farm drains and lakes – even in the high
country. It eats fish, freshwater crayfish and shellfish and can dive to at least
12 metres, often staying under for 20 seconds. The record is 58 seconds. It
can swallow eels well over half a metre long. Fishermen overseas fit the
bird with a collar to prevent it swallowing, and use this shag to catch fish.
It nests in large groups, mostly in trees. Also called great cormorant.
This subspecies is found also in New Guinea and Australia.

SEASHORE

For easy comparison, the colour art on these two pages is all to the same scale: SIXTH LIFE-SIZE

◆ Neck, legs and bill all very long
◆ IN FLIGHT: Broad wings, neck folded back, legs trailing, slow wingbeats

Herons stand or wade slowly in shallow water, stabbing their long bills at fish and other water creatures.

Reef Heron / Matuku Tai

Egretta sacra [Ardeidae]

Native	
Not common (5)	
400g	66cm

- Small heron, often hunched
- When feeding, sometimes shades the water with its outspread wings
- Flies close to the water

◆ Dark grey body *(much darker than other herons)*

More common in the North Island, mostly on the rocky shore, but often visiting firm mudflats. When the tide is out, it hunts (day or night) for fish, crabs and shellfish. It nests along rocky coasts, under overhangs and in caves. Found also from Bangladesh to Japan, Australia and the Pacific Islands. In Asia, where the bird is usually white, it is known as the sacred egret. It can live to 14 years old. Matuku is a general Māori name for herons.

◆ White face *(unlike reef heron)*

White-Faced Heron / Matuku Moana

Ardea novaehollandiae [Ardeidae]

Native	
Very common (45)	
550g	67cm

- Common on farmland & the coast
- *Stands more upright than reef heron*
- Harsh flight call: 'kraaah'
- In flight, wings two-toned *(unlike reef heron – above)*

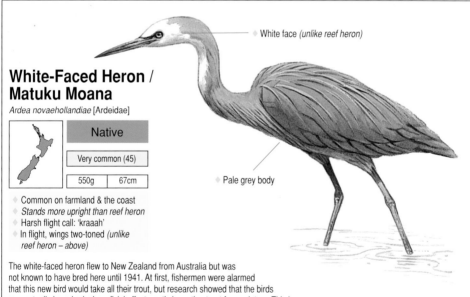

◆ Pale grey body

The white-faced heron flew to New Zealand from Australia but was not known to have bred here until 1941. At first, fishermen were alarmed that this new bird would take all their trout, but research showed that the birds may actually have had a beneficial effect, partly by eating trout fry predators. This is now New Zealand's most common heron, its success here being due to its wide range of food and habitat. Indeed, it is now more common here than in Australia. It is common in estuaries, rivers, lakes and farmland, often nesting in clumps of pine or gum trees and can often be seen perching on fenceposts or cattle troughs, or even in town parks. In estuaries it is sometimes seen raking one foot in the water to stir up water creatures to eat. Its food includes fish, frogs, tadpoles, insects, worms and mice. Found also in Indonesia, New Guinea and Australia.

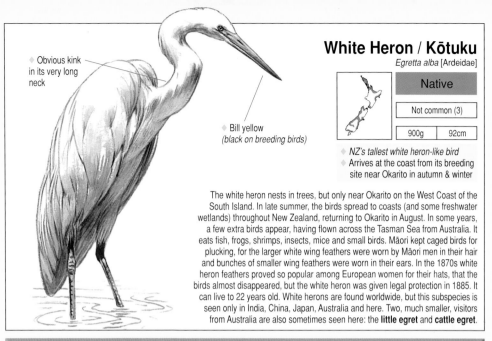

White Heron / Kōtuku
Egretta alba [Ardeidae]

◆ Obvious kink in its very long neck

◆ Bill yellow *(black on breeding birds)*

Native	
Not common (3)	
900g	92cm

◆ *NZ's tallest white heron-like bird*
◆ Arrives at the coast from its breeding site near Okarito in autumn & winter

The white heron nests in trees, but only near Okarito on the West Coast of the South Island. In late summer, the birds spread to coasts (and some freshwater wetlands) throughout New Zealand, returning to Okarito in August. In some years, a few extra birds appear, having flown across the Tasman Sea from Australia. It eats fish, frogs, shrimps, insects, mice and small birds. Māori kept caged birds for plucking, for the larger white wing feathers were worn by Māori men in their hair and bunches of smaller wing feathers were worn in their ears. In the 1870s white heron feathers proved so popular among European women for their hats, that the birds almost disappeared, but the white heron was given legal protection in 1885. It can live to 22 years old. White herons are found worldwide, but this subspecies is seen only in India, China, Japan, Australia and here. Two, much smaller, visitors from Australia are also sometimes seen here: the **little egret** and **cattle egret**.

Seashore Birds: Spoonbills   Tall Birds with Long Legs

◆ Wide spoon-shaped bill for scooping food from the water surface
◆ IN FLIGHT: Fast wingbeats, neck extended *(unlike true herons)*

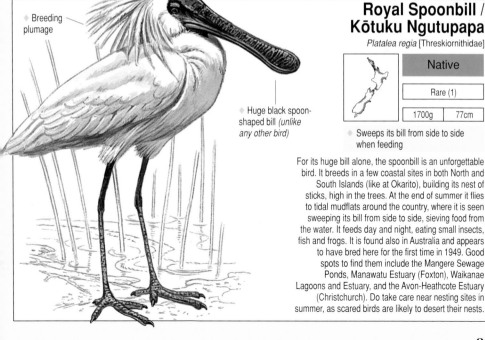

Royal Spoonbill / Kōtuku Ngutupapa
Platalea regia [Threskiornithidae]

◆ Breeding plumage

◆ Huge black spoon-shaped bill *(unlike any other bird)*

Native	
Rare (1)	
1700g	77cm

◆ Sweeps its bill from side to side when feeding

For its huge bill alone, the spoonbill is an unforgettable bird. It breeds in a few coastal sites in both North and South Islands (like at Okarito), building its nest of sticks, high in the trees. At the end of summer it flies to tidal mudflats around the country, where it is seen sweeping its bill from side to side, sieving food from the water. It feeds day and night, eating small insects, fish and frogs. It is found also in Australia and appears to have bred here for the first time in 1949. Good spots to find them include the Mangere Sewage Ponds, Manawatu Estuary (Foxton), Waikanae Lagoons and Estuary, and the Avon-Heathcote Estuary (Christchurch). Do take care near nesting sites in summer, as scared birds are likely to desert their nests.

SEASHORE

Seashore Birds: Penguins

The world's largest ever penguin, the **New Zealand giant penguin**, weighed around 100 kg and stood about 1.5 m tall, but died out about 40 million years ago. These days, New Zealand has 13 of the world's 16 penguin species, but most are rare or are found only on the subantarctic islands.

Blue Penguin / Korora
Eudyptula minor [Spheniscidae]

Blue-grey back

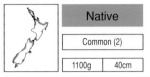

Native
Common (2)

| 1100g | 40cm |

- Usually spotted at sea in calm weather
- Comes ashore at night especially August-March
- Noisy on land at night, or at sea at dusk

New Zealand's most common penguin and the only penguin breeding along North Island coasts. It is also the world's smallest penguin. It is usually spotted swimming on its own or in small groups, spending most of the year at sea – even sleeping on the water – but often coming ashore at night to rest. It hunts small squid, fish and octopus. Some years, around Christmas, large numbers are washed ashore, but the reason for this is not known. From about August onwards, they return to land to breed in burrows, caves, or under driftwood, also under beach cottages and boatsheds. They usually nest near the coast, but can travel a kilometre or more inland, sometimes climbing steep cliff faces. Road signs warn motorists to watch out at night for birds crossing the road to reach their nests. Signs on beaches help explain the need to keep dogs and cats away from these areas (especially at night). Visit the beach at dawn to spot their foot and flipper tracks in the sand from the previous night. From late December to March, birds come ashore again for up to two weeks to moult in caves. At this time, holiday makers often think the birds are sick and try to rescue them, for moulting penguins can look very scruffy. A moulting penguin replaces its feathers all at once, so is unable to swim or eat for these two weeks. Keep an eye out for them from the inter-island ferry. They are good swimmers; though small, one swam 113 km in 24 hours. They can also dive to depths of at least 69 metres, Blue penguins can live to over 19 years old. It is the only penguin to breed on the coast of mainland Australia. Their colouring varies from place to place, the most distinctive form being the **white-flippered penguin** of Banks Peninsula.

Yellow-Eyed Penguin / Hoiho
Megadyptes antipodes [Spheniscidae]

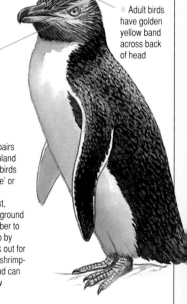

Adult birds have golden yellow band across back of head

Yellow eye

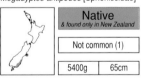

Native
& found only in New Zealand
Not common (1)

| 5400g | 65cm |

- **Not in the North Island**
- Comes ashore throughout the year
- Trumpeting calls from nest site

Most penguins live in noisy groups, or colonies, among rocks, or on snow and ice, but pairs of hoiho make for secluded forest and scrub to nest. This – New Zealand's largest mainland penguin – is endangered and one of the rarest penguins in the world, with about 5,000 birds left. Nonetheless, the yellow-eyed penguin can easily be seen by visiting 'Penguin Place' or 'Southlight Wildlife', near Taiaroa Head on the Otago Peninsula (not far from the Royal albatross colony), for they come ashore daily throughout the year. Late afternoon is best, when the birds are returning. The birds climb over rocky or sandy beaches and difficult ground to reach their nesting sites (up to 1 km inland) south of Banks Peninsula. From September to October, they lay their pale bluish-green eggs in a hollow in the ground. Volunteers help by excluding dogs and stock from nesting sites, trapping ferrets, stoats and wild cats. Look out for this penguin from the ferry to Stewart Island. It eats fish, squid, octopus and krill (small shrimp-like creatures). It can accurately find its way home over distances of 350 km or more and can live to over 30 years old. (The similar **Fiordland crested penguin** – with a bright yellow stripe above the eye – is sometimes seen between Haast and Milford.)

This gannet breeds only in Australia, Norfolk Island and New Zealand. A different species is found in the North Atlantic and a third one is seen around the coasts of southern Africa to Australia.

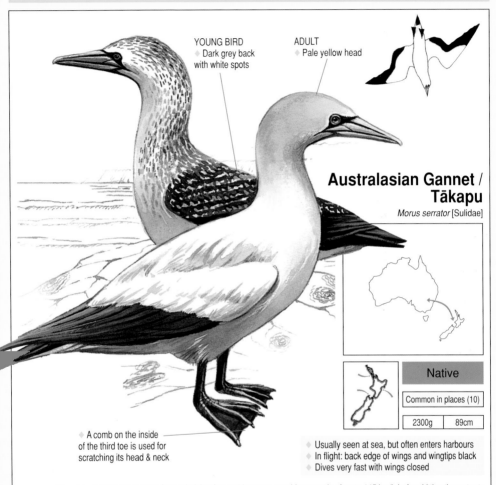

YOUNG BIRD
◆ Dark grey back with white spots

ADULT
◆ Pale yellow head

Australasian Gannet / Tākapu
Morus serrator [Sulidae]

Native

Common in places (10)

| 2300g | 89cm |

◆ A comb on the inside of the third toe is used for scratching its head & neck

◆ Usually seen at sea, but often enters harbours
◆ In flight: back edge of wings and wingtips black
◆ Dives very fast with wings closed

The gannet drops like a stone from a height of up to 30 metres, reaching speeds of up to 145 km/h before hitting the water to reach depths of up to 8 metres. To avoid getting hurt, it collapses its wings and inflates shock cushions on its lower neck and chest. In 1974, one dived onto a car crossing the Auckland Harbour Bridge. Although it broke the car windscreen, the dead bird's head and neck survived the impact. It feeds several kilometres out to sea, but also close to shore, diving for fish and squid. It nests mostly on offshore islands around the northern half of the North Island. New Zealand is a good place to see gannets because there are accessible mainland breeding colonies – at Muriwai (near Auckland), Cape Kidnappers (Hawke Bay) and Farewell Spit (in the north of the South Island). The birds can be seen here from July to January, offering a chance to see their fascinating courtship rituals, their take-off from the cliff, their feeding, fighting, calling and brooding. Binoculars are useful but certainly not essential. Take care as breeding birds are easily disturbed. Bowl-shaped nests made from seaweed and bird droppings are spaced in a regular pattern about 1 metre apart, each bird laying just one blue-green egg. The chick grows fast and, with its thick layer of down, soon looks much larger than its parents. In late December and January, almost all the young birds leave for eastern and southern Australia, not returning to New Zealand until 3-7 years old. They return in June or July, although some of the younger birds don't survive the long crossing and are found washed up along northern beaches. If they survive this ordeal, they can live to over 30 years old. Gannet feathers are among those traditionally worn by Māori in their hair. To celebrate the Christmas of 1769 during Cook's first voyage to New Zealand, these birds were baked in a pie. The same bird breeds also in the Norfolk Islands and Australia.

SEASHORE

Albatrosses range from twice the size of a black-backed gull to nine times this size. They have long narrow wings, a short tail, and a long heavy bill with nostril tubes at the top. Most are dark above, white below. All soar with stiffly held wings and only rarely need to flap them. Ten of the world's 14 albatrosses are found in the New Zealand region. (To be more exact, the current estimate for the world total of albatross species lies somewhere between 14 and 24, depending on the taxonomist.) The smaller one are commonly known as **mollymawks**. The largest is the royal albatross shown here.

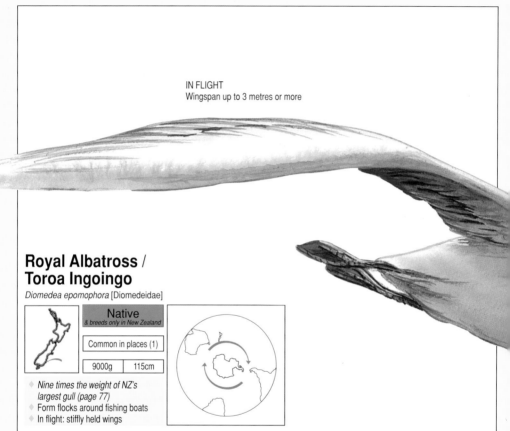

IN FLIGHT
Wingspan up to 3 metres or more

Royal Albatross / Toroa Ingoingo

Diomedea epomophora [Diomedeidae]

Native
& breeds only in New Zealand
Common in places (1)
9000g	115cm

- Nine times the weight of NZ's largest gull (page 77)
- Form flocks around fishing boats
- In flight: stiffly held wings

One of the largest flying birds in the world, the royal albatross can have a wingspan of over three metres. It breeds only in New Zealand and its outlying islands, but rides the circumpolar winds to feed on squid in seas off South America, returning along a route to the south of Africa and Australia, back again to New Zealand. Nesting birds can be seen year round (except 16 Sept–24 Nov) at the only mainland albatross-breeding colony in the world: from an observatory at Taiaroa Head on the Otago Peninsula, near Dunedin. (The other royals breed on the Chatham Islands, Campbell and Auckland Islands.) It lays one large egg (as big as a kiwi egg – see page 91) and incubation lasts almost three months. It is not until the chicks are eight months old that they can fly and look after themselves, so the whole chick-rearing process takes nearly the whole year. This means that successful parents can only breed once every two years. When ready to fly, the chick makes no practice flights and simply steps off the cliff into the wind. It will not walk on land again for 3-6 years and will spend more than 80 percent of its life at sea. Famed for its long-distance gliding, it simply locks its wings in place, using a special tendon, hardly using a wingbeat for thousands of kilometres. It flies at speeds of up to 115 km/hr, swooping at up to 140 km/hr or more. To take off from the sea, it flaps its wings and paddles furiously, running over the top of the water into the wind to get started. A good place to watch out for royal albatrosses in flight is from the inter-island ferry – especially if you are travelling in winter. The current record for the world's oldest seabird is held by one royal albatross called 'Grandma' who was estimated to be more than 62 years old. Māori caught albatrosses for food and for their feathers which were used for cloak-making, for personal decoration, or to beautify canoes and food containers. The bones were used to make spear tips, nose flutes and toggles. The similar-looking **wandering albatross** – also found in New Zealand waters – holds the record for the world's longest wingspan of any living bird: 3.63 metres.

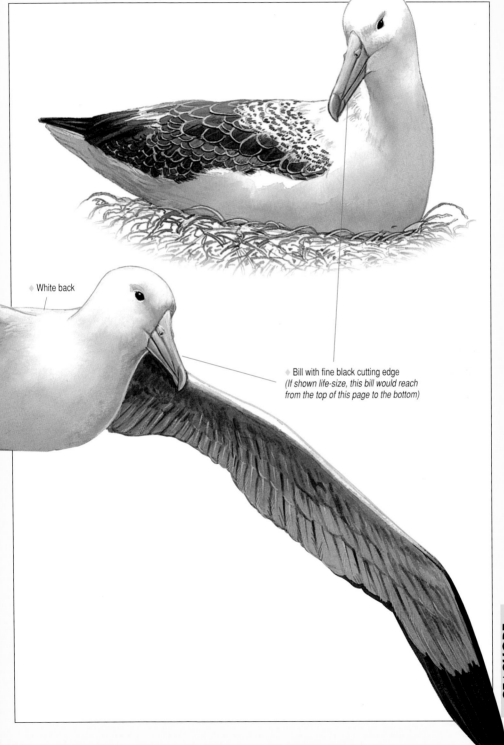

◆ White back

◆ Bill with fine black cutting edge
*(If shown life-size, this bill would reach
from the top of this page to the bottom)*

Birds by Size

If you can't find the bird by habitat, you can also look up any bird by **size**. There is no need to know its exact size. Just find a similar-sized bird you are familiar with in this list and work your way up or down from there. For example, is your bird the size (bulk) of a **sparrow**, **blackbird**, **city pigeon** or a **common duck**? The colours show the habitat where each bird is most likely to be found (as follows):

■ Forest ■ Sanctuary ■ Mountain ■ Countryside & Garden ■ Freshwater ■ Seashore

weight in grams		page
6.5	Rifleman	8
6.5	Grey Warbler	8
8	Fantail	9
11	Tomtit	9
12	Redpoll	36
12	Brown Creeper	10
13	Silvereye	10
14	Swallow	54
16	Goldfinch	37
17	Whitehead	11
18	Rock Wren	28
21	Dunnock	38
22	Chaffinch	38
25	Shining Cuckoo	12
27	Yellowhammer	39
28	Greenfinch	39
28	Yellowhead	12
30	**House Sparrow**	40
30	Bellbird	13
35	NZ Robin	13
35	Fernbird	54
35	Stitchbird	23
38	Skylark	41
40	Pipit	41
45	Spotless Crake	55
45	Yellow-Crowned Parakeet	14
60	Wrybill	72
60	Banded Dotterel	72
65	Kingfisher	55
70	Song Thrush	42
75	Saddleback	23
80	Black-Fronted Tern	56
85	Starling	42
90	**Blackbird**	43
105	Tūī	15
110	Rosella	44
120	Lesser Knot	73
125	Myna	44
125	Long-Tailed Cuckoo	16
160	NZ Dotterel	73
160	White-Fronted Tern	74
170	Banded Rail	56
175	Morepork	16
180	Little Owl	45
180	California Quail	45
190	Pied Stilt	74
230	Kōkako	17
250	Dabchick	57

weight in grams		page
275	Black-Billed Gull	57
280	Red-Billed Gull	75
325	Bar-Tailed Godwit	75
350	Australian Magpie	46
360	Spur-Winged Plover	46
400	**City Pigeon**	47
400	Falcon	17
400	Rook	47
400	Reef Heron	80
475	Grey Teal	58
500	Kākā	18
545	Coot	58
550	Pied Oystercatcher	76
550	White-Faced Heron	80
550	Chukor	48
625	Shoveler	59
650	Scaup	59
650	NZ Pigeon	19
700	Caspian Tern	76
700	Little Shag	78
725	Variable Oystercatcher	77
750	Harrier	48
800	Little Black Shag	78
825	Blue Duck	60
850	Weka	20
900	Kea	29
900	White Heron	81
950	Pūkeko	60
950	Black-Backed Gull	77
1050	Grey Duck	61
1100	Crested Grebe	61
1100	Blue Penguin	82
1200	**Common Duck**	62
1200	Spotted Shag	79
1200	Australasian Bittern	64
1300	Pheasant	49
1550	Paradise Shelduck	62
1700	Royal Spoonbill	81
2000	Pied Shag	79
2200	Black Shag	79
2250	Kākāpō	24
2300	Gannet	83
2500	Brown Kiwi	21
3000	Takahē	25
4950	Canada Goose	65
5400	Yellow-Eyed Penguin	82
5500	Black Swan	66
9000	Royal Albatross	84

Because some birds have a very long tail, neck or bill (making it hard to compare bird sizes), weights are listed instead of lengths. If male and female birds are different sizes, the average weight is listed.

Birds by Colour

(The birds in each group are listed in order of size, starting with the smallest. Sanctuary birds excluded.)

RAINBOW-COLOURED	page
Rosella (& Rainbow Lorikeet)	44

BRIGHT RED	page
Redpoll (on chest of male)	36
Goldfinch (on face)	37
Rosella (head)	44
Pūkeko (crown & bill)	60
Pheasant (on face of male)	49

YELLOW	page
Goldfinch (on wings)	37
Yellowhammer (on head & chest)	39
Greenfinch (on wings)	39
Yellowhead (South Island forest only)	12
Spur-Winged Plover (on face)	46

GREEN	page
Rifleman (male)	8
Silvereye (with white eye ring)	10
Shining Cuckoo (with white stripes)	12
Greenfinch (olive green)	39
Bellbird (olive green)	13
Parakeet (bright green forest parrot)	14
NZ Pigeon (with white singlet)	19
Kea (South Island only)	29

BLUE	page
Swallow (blue-black head & back)	54
Kingfisher (bright blue back)	55
Pūkeko (with red crown & bill)	60

ALL BLACK	page
Starling (iridescent in sunlight)	42
Blackbird (male)	43
Tūī (iridescent in sunlight)	15
Rook (a large crow)	47
Coot (lake bird with white beak & forehead)	58
Scaup (lake bird)	59
Variable Oystercatcher (long red bill)	77
Shags (long neck)	78-79
Black Swan (long neck)	66

ALL WHITE	page
White Heron, Spoonbill (& Cattle Egret)	81

BLACK & WHITE	page
Tomtit (forest bird)	9
Pied Stilt (long bill & long legs)	74
Magpie (large crow-like bird)	46
Oystercatchers (long orange-red bill)	76-77
Black-Backed Gull (NZ's largest seagull)	77
Little Shag & Pied Shag (long neck)	78-79

Birds with a very long bill, neck, legs or tail

(The birds in each group are listed in order of size, starting with the smallest.)

VERY LONG BILL (longer than head)	page
Kingfisher (bright blue back)	55
Pied Stilt (slender black & white bird)	74
Godwit (upturned bill)	75
Oystercatchers (orange-red bill)	76-77
Herons & Spoonbill (tall)	80-81
Bittern (tall swamp bird)	64
Kiwi (flightless night-time forest bird)	21

VERY LONG NECK	page
Pied Stilt (with long legs)	74
Shags (tall, with short legs)	78-79
Herons & Spoonbill (with long legs)	80-81
Geese & Swans (lake birds)	65-66

VERY LONG LEGS	page
Pied Stilt (black & white bird)	74
Godwit (upturned bill)	75
Pūkeko (dark blue with red bill)	60
Herons & Spoonbill (very tall birds)	80-81
Bittern (tall swamp bird)	64

VERY LONG TAIL (as long as body)	page
Fantail (fan-shaped tail)	9
Fernbird (hidden in low scrub)	54
Parakeet (bright green forest parrot)	14
Rosella (rainbow-coloured parrot)	44
Long-Tailed Cuckoo (brown forest bird)	16
Pheasant (very large; poor flier)	49

A Simple Key to Bird Groups

A simplified guide to the main New Zealand families and orders.

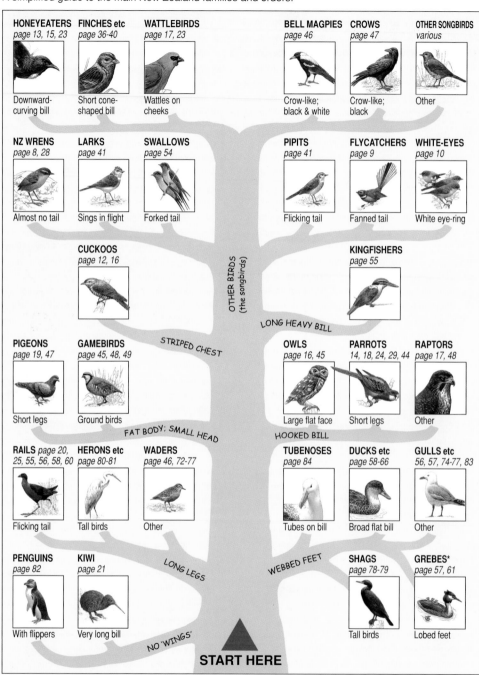

HONEYEATERS
page 13, 15, 23
Downward-curving bill

FINCHES etc
page 36-40
Short cone-shaped bill

WATTLEBIRDS
page 17, 23
Wattles on cheeks

BELL MAGPIES
page 46
Crow-like; black & white

CROWS
page 47
Crow-like; black

OTHER SONGBIRDS
various
Other

NZ WRENS
page 8, 28
Almost no tail

LARKS
page 41
Sings in flight

SWALLOWS
page 54
Forked tail

PIPITS
page 41
Flicking tail

FLYCATCHERS
page 9
Fanned tail

WHITE-EYES
page 10
White eye-ring

CUCKOOS
page 12, 16

KINGFISHERS
page 55

OTHER BIRDS (the songbirds)

LONG HEAVY BILL

STRIPED CHEST

PIGEONS
page 19, 47
Short legs

GAMEBIRDS
page 45, 48, 49
Ground birds

OWLS
page 16, 45
Large flat face

PARROTS
14, 18, 24, 29, 44
Short legs

RAPTORS
page 17, 48
Other

FAT BODY; SMALL HEAD

HOOKED BILL

RAILS *page 20, 25, 55, 56, 58, 60*
Flicking tail

HERONS etc
page 80-81
Tall birds

WADERS
page 46, 72-77
Other

TUBENOSES
page 84
Tubes on bill

DUCKS etc
page 58-66
Broad flat bill

GULLS etc
56, 57, 74-77, 83
Other

PENGUINS
page 82
With flippers

KIWI
page 21
Very long bill

LONG LEGS

WEBBED FEET

SHAGS
page 78-79
Tall birds

GREBES*
page 57, 61
Lobed feet

NO 'WINGS'

START HERE

For this key to work, you need to start at the bottom of the page.   (*Although a coot has lobed feet, it is a rail.*)

Bird Eggs

This guide is designed to help people identify abandoned eggs. Note that touching an egg or chick in its nest may make the parent bird desert the nest. To identify these eggs, simply hide nearby and watch for the parent to return. The welfare of the birds must come first. Note too that collecting eggs of native or game birds is illegal. New Zealand's most commonly found bird eggs are shown here at exactly life size, arranged from the smallest to the largest.

Redpoll
page 36

Fantail
page 9

Goldfinch
page 37

Grey Warbler
page 8

Silvereye
page 10

Welcome Swallow
page 54

Shining Cuckoo
page 12

Chaffinch
page 38

Dunnock
page 38

Yellowhammer
page 39

Greenfinch
page 39

House Sparrow
page 40

Bellbird
page 13

NZ Pipit
page 41

Skylark
page 41

Song Thrush
page 42

Blackbird
page 43

Tūī
page 15

Myna
page 44

Starling
page 42

California Quail
page 45

(All eggs shown life-size)

Australian Magpie
page 46

Pied Stilt
page 74

Pheasant
page 49

Spur-Winged Plover
page 46

NZ Pigeon
page 19

Pūkeko
page 60

Red-Billed Gull
page 75

Variable Oystercatcher
page 77

Mallard Duck
page 62

(All eggs shown life-size)

Black-Backed Gull
page 77

Brown Kiwi
page 21

(All eggs shown life-size)

Birdwatching Hot Spots

Recommended and readily accessible hot spots for beginners' birdwatching are shown in bold type. Other important bird sites are shown in light print.

North Island

1. **Aroha Island Ecological Centre**, Rangitane *(kiwi)*
2. **Trounson Kauri Park** *(kiwi)*
3. **Wenderholm Regional Park** *(banded rail, bush birds)*
4. **Wade (Weiti) River** *(shorebirds)*
5. **Tiritiri Matangi Island** *(sanctuary birds)*
6. **Kawau Island** *(weka, kookaburra)*
7. Little Barrier Island (DoC permit required)
8. Kaipara Harbour, nr Tapora *(shorebirds)*
9. **Muriwai Beach** *(gannet)*
10. Manukau Harbour *(shorebirds)*
11. **Miranda Shorebird Centre** *(shorebirds)*
12. Tauranga Harbour *(shorebirds)*
13. **Kaituna Estuary,** Maketu *(waterfowl, shorebirds)*
14. **Matata Lagoons** *(wetland birds, shorebirds)*
15. **Rotorua Lakes** *(waterfowl, bush birds)*
16. **Mokoia Island,** in Lake Rotorua *(stitchbird & saddleback)*
17. **Otorohanga Kiwi House** *(native bird displays)*
18. **Pureora Forest (tower)** *(bush birds)*
19. **Atiamuri Pine Forests** *(bush birds)*
20. Whirinaki Forest *(bush birds)*
21. **Opepe Historic Reserve,** SH 5 *(bush birds)*
22. **Waikareiti Track,** Lake Waikaremoana *(bush birds)*
23. **Pukeiti Rhododendron Trust** *(bush birds)*
24. **Taurewa Walk,** Taurewa *(bush birds)*
25. **Tokaanu,** Lake Taupo *(waterfowl, crake, fernbird)*
26. **Lake Rotopounamu** *(bush birds)*
27. **Cape Kidnappers** *(gannet)*
28. **Manawatu Estuary,** Foxton *(shorebirds)*
29. **Waikanae Lagoons & Estuary** *(waterfowl, shorebirds)*
    & Nga Manu Nature Reserve, Waikanae *(native bird displays)*
30. **Mt Bruce Wildlife Centre** *(native bird displays)*
31. **Kapiti Island** (DoC permission required)
31a.**Karori Wildlife Sanctuary** *(bush and sanctuary birds)*
32. **Interisland Ferry** *(seabirds)*

KEY TO BIRDWATCHING HABITATS
- Forest birds
- Sanctuary birds
- Mountain birds
- Freshwater birds
- Seashore birds

South Island

33. Farewell Spit *(shorebirds)*
34. Maud Island (DoC permission required)
35. **Motuara Island** *(saddleback, bush birds)*
36. **Lake Rotoiti** *(bush birds)*
37. **Kaikoura** *(seabirds)*
38. St Anne's Lagoon, Cheviot *(waterfowl, wetland birds)*
39. Lake Brunner *(great spotted kiwi)*
40. Lake Kaniere *(falcon, waterfowl)*
41. **Arthur's Pass** *(bush birds, rock wren, kea, blue duck)*
42. **Avon-Heathcote Estuary** *(waterfowl, shorebirds)*
43. Lake Ellesmere *(waterfowl)*
44. Rakaia, Rangitata & Waitaki Rivers *(riverbed birds)*
45. Whataroa, nr Okarito *(white heron, spoonbill)*
46. Lake Mapourika *(grebe, scaup)*
47. Franz Joseph & Fox Glacier *(kea, bush birds)*
48. **Haast Pass & Makarora** *(yellowhead, falcon, bush birds)*
49. Lakes Alexandrina & McGregor *(crested grebe)*
50. **Black Stilt Aviary,** Twizel *(black stilt)*
51. Ahuriri River *(riverbed birds)*
52. **Homer Tunnel** & Gertrude Saddle *(rock wren, kea)*
53. **Eglinton Valley & Lake Gunn Track** *(falcon, bush birds)*
54. **Te Anau Wildlife Centre** *(native bird displays)*
55. Redcliff Wetland Reserve *(waterfowl, crake)*
56. **Oamaru** *(penguin)*
57. **Otago Peninsula** *(albatross & penguin)*
58. **Sinclair Wetlands,** Lake Waihola *(waterfowl, fernbird)*
59. **Nugget Point** *(seabirds)*
60. Waituna Lagoon & Awarua Bay *(shorebirds)*

61. **Stewart Island** *(kiwi, bush birds, seabirds)*
62. Codfish Island (DoC permission required)

Further Reading

Chambers, Stuart. *Birds of New Zealand Locality Guide*. Arun Books, Hamilton, 1989.
(A practical guide to the best places to see each species.)
Ell, Gordon. *Encouraging Birds in the New Zealand Garden.*
The Bush Press, Auckland, 1981.
Ellis, Brian. *The New Zealand Birdwatchers' Book*. Reed Methuen, Auckland, 1987.
Hayman, Piers. *The Bird Next Door*. New Holland, Auckland, 1999. (In question-
and-answer format, covers many commonly asked questions about birds.)
Heather, Barrie D. & Hugh A. Robertson. *The Field Guide to the Birds of New Zealand*.
Penguin, Auckland, 1996. (A complete and up-to-date reference to every bird
seen in the wild in New Zealand.)
Moon, Geoff. *A Field Guide to New Zealand Birds*. Reed, Auckland, 1992.
(With photographs.)
Oliver, W. R. B. *New Zealand Birds*. Reed, Wellington, 1930 (2nd ed 1955).
(Very detailed although long out of print.)
Robertson, C. J. R. (Ed.) *Complete Book of New Zealand Birds*. Reader's Digest, Sydney,
1985. (Excellent photographs with very detailed background information.)

Useful Websites

Yellow-Eyed Penguin Trust	www.yellow-eyedpenguin.org.nz
Royal Forest & Bird Protection Society	www.forest-bird.org.nz
Department of Conservation	www.doc.govt.nz
Kiwi Recovery Programme	www.kiwirecovery.org.nz
Supporters of Tiritiri Matangi	www.tiritirimatangi.org.nz
The Ornithological Society of New Zealand	www.nzbirds.com
Kakapo Recovery Programme	www.kakaporecovery.org.nz
Aroha Island Ecological Reserve	www.aroha.net.nz
Mount Bruce National Wildlife Centre	www.mtbruce.doc.govt.nz
Royal Albatross Centre	www.albatrosses.org.nz
Miranda Shorebird Centre	www.miranda-shorebird.org.nz
Ngā Manu Nature Reserve, Waikanae	www.ngamanu.co.nz
Karori Wildlife Sanctuary, Karori	www.sanctuary.org.nz

Clubs

The Ornithological Society of New Zealand, P.O. Box 12397, Wellington.
Royal Forest & Bird Protection Society, P.O. Box 631, Wellington.
Miranda Naturalists' Trust, R.D. 3, Pokeno.
Yellow-Eyed Penguin Trust, P.O. Box 5409, Dunedin.
Karori Wildlife Sanctuary Trust, P.O. Box 9267, Wellington
Friend of Ngā Manu, P.O. Box 126, Waikanae.
Supporters of Tiritiri Matangi, P.O. Box 90-814, Auckland.

Encouragement to Children

Why not set up a birdwatching club at school or at home? Parents: a simple word of encouragement can make all the difference. Take the children to a birdwatcher's slide show meeting or on a field trip. Help them fundraise or save up for binoculars.

Choosing Binoculars

For birdwatching, a typical specification is 8 x 30. The first figure shows magnification (8x); the second shows lens diameter (30 mm) – giving an indication of how wide the field of view is. A narrow field of view (eg 8 x 20) can make it tricky to 'get a fix on' the bird, especially if the bird keeps moving. More than 10x magnification can be hard to hold steady. So the magnification should generally be 8–10x and lens width 30–50 mm. To tell if they are a good pair, try them out in natural light on a dull day. It is worth taking time to find a pair which you find comfortable to use. A wide neckstrap helps.

Māori Bird Names

769 Māori bird names (including tribal variations) are listed below under their standard common English names.

albatross, light-mantled sooty
kōputu, toroa haunui, toroa pango, toroa ruru, toroa-a-ruru

albatross, royal
toroa ingoingo, toroa whakaingo, toroa whakairo[7]

albatross, wandering
toroa, toroa teoteo[6] (when young)

bellbird
tītapu [Bay of Plenty] or tōtōaireka (both female), kēkerematua or kerekerematātu (both male), kohimako, kōhoimako, kōhorimako, kōkōmako, kōkorihimako, kōkorimako, kōkorohimako, kōkoromako, kōmako, kōmakohua[7], kōmakohuariki[7] (dominant male), kōmamako, kōpaopao, kōpara, kōparapara, korihako, korimako, koromako, kotaiahu, mako, makomako, para, rearea, tītīmako, titimoko[5], titōmako, tukumako, tutumako

bittern, Australasian
hūrepo, hūroto, kāka, kautuku, matuku, matuku-hūrepo, matuku-kāka

bittern, New Zealand little (extinct)
kaoriki, kioriki

blackbird (introduced)
manu pango[4]

chaffinch (introduced)
pahirini[4], whitira korepe[4]

crake, marsh
kāreke, koitareke, kōkōreke, koreke, kōriki, kotoreke

crake, spotless
kueto, kūweto, pūeto, pūetoeto, pūtoto, pūweto, pūwetoweto

creeper, brown
pīpipi, pipirihika, tītirihika, toitoi

cuckoo, long-tailed
kaweau, kawekaweā, kawekaweau, koehoperoa, koekoeā, koekoeau, kōhoperoa, kokoea, kuekuea

cuckoo, shining
piripiriwharauroa, Te Manu a Māui [Ngāitahu], nakonako, pīpīauroa, pipiriwharauroa, pīpīwharauroa, whakarauroa, wharauroa, wharauroa whēnakonako

dabchick, New Zealand
taihoropi [Ngāpuhi], taratimoho [Waikato], tokitoki, tokitokipia, tokitokipio, tongitongipia, totoipio, totokipia, totokipio, weiweia, weweia, whirowhiro

dotterel, banded
piopio, pohowera, turiwhati, turiwhatu, tūturiwhatu[283]

dotterel, New Zealand
kūkuruatu, pukunui, rako, tākahikahi, tākaikaha, tākaikai, turiwhati, turiwhatu, turuatu, turuturuwhatu, turuwhatu, tūturiwhati, tūturiwhatu, tuturuatu, tūturuwhatu

duck, blue
korowhio, whio, whiorau

duck, grey
topatopa (ducklings only?), parera [Ngāpuhi,

Waikato], karakahia, māunu, pārera, tāwaka

duck, white-eyed
karakahia[3]

falcon, New Zealand
kakarapiti (male), kāeaea, kāiaia, kaiawa, kāieie, kārearea, kārewarewa, kārewarewa tara, kāuaua, tāwaka

fantail
hirairaka, hītakataka, hīwaiwaka, hīwakawaka, kōtiutiu, pīrairaka, pīrakaraka, pīrangirangi, pitakataka, pīwaiwaka, pīwakawaka, tīaiaka, tīaka, tīakaaka, tieaka, tīrairaka, tīrakaraka, tīraureka, tītakataka, tītīrairaka, tīwaiwaka, tīwakawaka, wakawaka

fernbird
koroātito, korowātito, kōtātā, kūkurutoki, mātā, mātātā, mātuhi, nako, ngako, toetoe, whetito, wetito

gannet, Australasian
karake, tākapu, tākupu, tākupu karake, tatakī, tātākī, toroa haoika, toroa horoika, toroa tatakī

godwit, bar-tailed
hakakao or kakao (an old bird), karoro (in a particular plumage), Pāerarera (juvenile), rakakao [Ngāpuhi], kuaka, kūaka, kuhikuhiwaka, rīrīwaka, tapukōrako, tara kakao

goose (introduced; in general)
kuihi[5]

grebe, Australasian crested
kāha, kāmana, manapou, pāteketeke, pūteketeke[5]

gull, black-backed
kaiē or koiro or kōtingotingo or ngōiro or ngoiro or punua (all juvenile), karoro, rāpunga

gull, black-billed
tarapunga[2]

gull, red-billed
akiaki, hakorā, karehākoa, katatē, makorā, taketake, tarā punga, tarapunga[5], mākora[4], tarāpua (?) [Taranaki]

harrier, Australasian
kāhu-kōrako (for very old bird), kāhu pōkere o te whenua or kāhu-pango (juvenile), kāho [Te Aroha], kāhu, kāhu-komokomo, kāhu-maiepa, kērangi, manu-tahae

heron, reef
kākatai, matuku-moana, matuku-nuia, matuku-tai, matuku-waitai, mātukutuku, tīkāka

heron, white
kōtuku

heron, white-faced
matuku-moana

huia (extinct)
huia, huianui (female)[7], paoke (when seen alone)

kaka
huripā or kākā kererū or kākā kōrako or kākā kura or kākā pipiwharauroa or kākā reko (all varieties of), tīaka or kākā kura or tatarikuha[7] (all a leader of a flock of), tātāapopo, or tāwaka (male), perehere [Ngāpuhi], karoro uri (when in dark plumage), karoro tea (when in light plumage), kēkētoi (when too fat to fly),

tarariki (with short beak, possibly the female), kākā, kōrī, kōriwhai

kakapo
kākāpō, kākātarapō, tarapō, tarepō, tātarapō

kea
kea, keha, keorangi, kia

kingfisher
kōkare[7], kōtare, kōtarepopo, kōtaretare

kiwi (in general)
kiwi, rire (juvenile)

kiwi, brown (& tokoeka)
rowi or tokoeka or tokoweka [all South Island], kiwi kura, kiwi nui, kiwi parure

kiwi, great spotted
kiwi karuwai, kiwi roa, kiwi roaroa, roa, roaroa

kiwi, little spotted
kiwi pukupuku

knot, lesser
huahou

kokako
hōkoko, hōngā, hōngē, kōkako, ōngā, ōngē, pakara

magpie, Australian (introduced)
makipae[4&5], timohina[4]

moa (extinct)
moa

mollymawk, black-browed
toroa

morepork
karu peho (large-eyed), koukou, peho, pehopeho, ruru, ruru-peho, rurururu

owl, laughing (extinct)
hakoke, kakaha, kopake[5], ruru whēkau, whēkau, whēkaukau

oystercatcher, pied
tōrea, tōrea tai

oystercatcher, variable
tōrea, tōrea pango (dark phase), tōrea tai

parakeet
kākāriki, kākāwaiariki, kākāwairiki, kākāwariki, kākawariki, kawariki, kawatere, porete, pōreterete, poroti[7], pōwhaitere, torete, tōreterete

penguin, blue
kororā

penguin, Fiordland crested
tawake[6], tawaki[6], tawhaki[5], pokotiwha

penguin, yellow-eyed
hoihoi[6 & 7], hoiho[7], takaraka[8]

petrel, black
karetai, kuia, ruru-tāiko, taiko, toanui, tuanui[5]

petrel, common diving
kuaka[2]

petrel, Cook's
tītī

petrel, giant
pāngurunguru[6], pāngarungaru[6]

petrel, grey
kuia

petrel, grey-backed storm
reoreo

petrel, grey-faced

---

[1] Names without numbers are from Williams, H. W. *A Dictionary of the Māori Language*. Government Printer, 1985.
[2] Turbott, E. G. (ed.) *Buller's Birds of New Zealand*. Whitcoulls, 1967.
[3] Heather, Barrie & Hugh Robertson. *The Field Guide to the Birds of New Zealand*. Viking, 1996.

94

õi
petrel, mottled
korure[3]
petrel, white-faced storm
takahikare, takahikare moana, takahikare rangi, takahikare raro
pheasant (introduced)
peihana[4&5]
pigeon, New Zealand
rupe (a large one), tarariki (a small one), karoro tangi harau (in poetry), kererū, kūkū, kūkupa [Northland], parea [Chatham Islands]
piopio (extinct)
koropio, korohea, korokio, piopio, tiutiu, tiutiukata
pipit, New Zealand
hīoi, kātaitai, manukāhaki, manukāwhaki, pīhoihoi, pīoioi, pīpipi-tai[7], whāioio, whīoi, whioi
plover, shore
kohutapu, tuturuatu
prion, Antarctic
totorore, whiroia
prion, broad-billed
pararā, pekehā, pepekehā
prion, fairy
tītī wainui
pukeko
pākura, pūkeko, tangata tawhito
quail (introduced; in general)
kuera[4]
quail, New Zealand (extinct)
kāreke, koikoiareke, koitareke, koitāreke, kokoreke, kokōreke, koreke, kōriki[1&5], koutareke, koweka, tāreke, tāwaka, tūpererū, whēwhī
rail, banded
katatai, kātātai, mioweka[5], moho, moho kākatai[5], moho kātātai, moho pango, moho pātātai, moho pererū, moho popotai, moho pūohotata, moho tātai, motarua, oho, ohomauri, pātātai, pepe, pōpōtai, pūohotata
rail, Dieffenbach's [Chatham Islands] (extinct)
moeriki, mehoriki[10]
rail, Hawkins [Chatham Islands] (extinct)
mehonui[10]
rail, Hutton's [Chatham Islands] (extinct)
mātirakahu
rifleman
kōrurerure (female), tāpahipare (male), hōutūtu, kikimutu, kikirimutu, kōhurehure, kotikotipa, kotikotipae, kōtipatipa, kōtītititi, momotawai, momoutu, mōutuutu, muhumuhu, pihipihi, pipiriki, piripiri, tītitipounamu, tītīpounamu[5], toirua, tokepiripiri [Bay of Plenty]
robin, New Zealand
mokorā (female), hātoitoi, kakaruwai, karae[7], karuai, karuwai, kātoitoi, kātuhituhi [Ngāitahu][7], mōioio, pie[7], piere, pīere, pīhaua, pīhere, pītoitoi, tariwai, taruwai, tātaruwai, tātāwai, tītiwahanui, toitoireka, toroire[7], tōtōrori[7], tōtōara, totoi, tōtōwai, tōtōwara, toutou, toutouwai, wheko-pō
saddleback
pūrourou, tiaki, tīeke, tīeke-rere, tīraueke, tīrauweke, tīraweke
scaup, New Zealand
kaiharopia, matamatapōuri, matapo,

matapōuri, pāpango, pārera matapouri, pōkeke, pūakiaki, raipo, tētē, tētēpango, tītipōrangi, tītitipō[7]
shag (in general)
houmea, kawau, kōau
shag, black
kawau pū, kawau tuawhenua, māpo[7], māpua, māpunga, matapu[7], pāpua
shag, little
kawau paka, kawau teoteo, kawau tīeke, pohotea, teoteo
shag, little black
kawau tuī
shag, pied
aroarotea, kāruhiruhi, kawau, kōau
shag, spotted
kawau pāteketeke, kawau tikitiki, pārekareka
shearwater, flesh-footed
toanui[3]
shearwater, fluttering
hākoakoa, hākuakua, pakahā
shearwater, short-tailed
hakoko[7], õi
shearwater, sooty
hakeke, hākēkeke, koakoa, õi, takakau, tītī, totorore
shelduck, paradise
pūpūtangi-ā-tama, pūpūtangi-ā-toa, pūtangitangi, pūtangitangi-ā-tama, pūtangitangi-ā-toa
shoveler, Australasian
kāhoho, kūkuruwhetū[6], kuruhenga, kuruwhengi, kuruwhengu, papaungūngu, pāteke, pūtaitai, tētē, wetawetangū
silvereye
hiraka, iringatau, kanohi mōwhiti, mōtengitengi, pihipihi, pīkaraihe, poporehe, tauhou, tauhōu, whiorangi
skua, brown
hākoakoa, hākuakua
snipe, New Zealand (Snares Island ssp)
tutukiwi
snipe, New Zealand (extinct ssp)[3&9]
hākuai[6], hākuikui[6], hākuwai[6] [all Ngāitahu], hākawai[3], hōkioi[6], hōkiwai[6], ōkioi[6], hōkio[6]
sparrow, house (introduced)
tiu[4]
spoonbill, royal
kōtuku-ngutupapa
starling (introduced)
tāringi[4&5]
stilt, black
tōrea pango [Arawa], toreāpango [Arawa], kakī, poaka, pōkākā[7], tūarahia
stilt, pied
poaka, popourangi[7], tōrea, turituri-pourewa, turuturu-pourewa, tuturi-pourewa, tuturu-pourewa, waewae tōrea[6] [Arawa]
stitchbird
matakiore or tihe-kiore or tihe-wai (female), kōtihe-wera or tihe-ora or tihe-wera (male), hihi, kōhihi, kōtihe, kōtihetihe, mōtihetihe, tihe, tiora, tioro, tīoro
swallow (introduced)
warou[5]
swan (introduced; in general)
wani[5], kakīanau[5]
takahe

moho, moho keo, moho rākau, moho rangi, takahē, takahea, tokohea
teal, brown
tētē, pāteke, tarawhatu, tei, tētēwhero, tokitoki
teal, grey
pohoriki, tētē, tētē-moroiti, tētē-wai
tern (in general)
tara
tern, black-fronted
tarapirohe [Ngāitahu], tarapiroe[3]
tern, Caspian
kāhawai, tarā nui, taranui, tara punga, tarā punga
tern, fairy
tara iti, tara teo, tara teoteo
tern, white-fronted
tara
tomtit
ngirunguru [South Island], hōmiromiro, kikitore, kikitori, kōmiromiro, Māui pōtiki, mīmiro, miromiro, mirumiru, pīmiromiro, pīmirumiru, pīngirunguru, pīpitore, pipitori, pīrangirangi, piropiro, tāne-te-waiora, toitoi
tropicbird, red-tailed
amokura, rakorakoa[7]
tui
kouwha (female in early summer), kōkōtea or teoteo (female), kōkōtaua or kōkōuri or tākaha or tute (male), kōkō, kōpūrehe, tūī
warbler, grey
hīrorirori, hōrirerire, kōrire, kōrirerire, kōriroriro, nonoroheke, nonoroheko, pītongatonga[5], rirerire, riretoro, riroriro, tōtoroie, tōtororire, whiranga-ā-tau
weka
weka pango (dark, South Island, form), hoā, weka
whitehead
hore, horehore, mōriorio, mōtengitengi, pōpokotea, (misspelt as pōpokatea), pōporoihewa, popotea, porihawa, poriporihewa, poupoutea, tātāeko, tātāeto, tātāhore, tātaiato, tātaihore, tātāngaeko, tātaranaeko, tātarangaeko, tātariheko, upokotea
wren, bush (extinct)
hurupounamu, mātuhi[2], mātuhituhi, mātuitui[7], pīwauwau, puano
wren, rock
hurupounamu[7], mātuitui[7]
wrybill
ngutu pare, ngutu parore[5&7]
yellowhead
hihipopokera, mohoua[5], mohua, mōhuahua, momohua
unidentified birds
hāweru, hikuhiku, humuhumu, hurukiwi, karae karikawa, kawau reoreo, kawau tatakī, kōkā, kōkōtai, koroire, kororī, korotai, korotau, kōtai, kōwhāwhā, kuakai, maimoa, manumea, moakirua, moakurarua, mohorīrīwai, mokākāweka, mū, ngongo, ngungu, parure, patahoro, penu, pihoriki, pohio, popourangi, pōreterete, pouākai, rauhamoa, tahora, tapoturangi, tapuku, tarahuki, tārewa, tawake, tiotio, toroa whara, toroire, tūkararoa, turiwhekoirangi

[4] Ngata, H. M. *English-Maori Dictionary*. Learning Media, 1993.   [5] Ryan, P.M. *The Reed Dictionary of Modern Māori*. Reed, 1995
[6] R. K. Rikihana (personal communication)   [7] Hirini Melbourne (personal communication)   [8] Yellow-eyed Penguin Trust
[9] Gill, Brian & Paul Martinson. *New Zealand's Extinct Birds*. Random, 1991.
[10] Tennyson, Alan and Paul Martinson. *Extinct Birds of New Zealand*. Te Papa Press, Wellington, 2006.
Where the tribal origin of the name is known, this is shown in square brackets.

Index (Birds shown in **bold** type are illustrated)